Scrumban Software Maintenance
5 Steps to Stop Starting and Start Finishing

Nagesh Rao

I am forever grateful to almighty. I thank my parents, my wife Bhavana, my son Tanay, and my sisters Nirmala and Vinaya, therefore I am.

Contents

Preface

Remember when you were a kid and you inherited a toy or bicycle from an older sibling? Most often, you didn't choose the hand-me-down, and most likely it was different from what you really wanted. But you were expected to pick it up and like it anyway. Imagine **Software Development** as the older sibling and **Software Maintenance** as the younger one. The methodologies, processes, and tools adopted in Software Maintenance have been inherited from Software Development. For example, the Waterfall model or Scrum may be appropriate for Software Development. Processes around cascading phases or time-boxed iterations, metrics such as Productivity, Cost of Quality, and Defect Injection Rate may be relevant to Software Development, but adapting them as-is to Software Maintenance is exactly like inheriting that unwanted toy or bicycle from your older sibling.

Software Development and Software Maintenance are distinctly different, with respect to the nature of work and execution of these activities. The work types, work sizes, workflow, required skills, and work stages are all different in Software Maintenance. The execution models that are in practice are primarily devised for software development work, and passed on to maintenance teams with the assumption that the work is similar. This mismatch in execution models has made Software Maintenance inefficient and ineffective. Therefore, it is prudent to look at the needs of Software Maintenance, and devise models, processes, and practices that suit its requirements.

The challenges faced by Software Maintenance in recent times have become more complex. The functionality of software has become intricate, leading to the advent of multiple technology layers.

- Supporting varied technologies across multiple layers requires a number of specific and specialized resources.
- The business landscape has become complex, necessitating a number of specialized teams or groups to work together to deliver software maintenance services.

This led to the emergence of multiple stakeholders across business and IT functions with conflicting priorities, which in turn resulted in jugglery of work requests. So many software maintenance work requests get delayed in this process. The business impact of a software change not moving into production has increased exponentially, causing additional stress on Software Maintenance teams, with their capacity stretched beyond limits.

All these challenges pose great hurdles for Software Maintenance teams; they frequently stop and start work, switch contexts from one work request to another, and try to traverse the work requests through several silos of cross-functional teams. Over time, several execution models have evolved to address these challenges. Most of these follow agile and Lean methodologies. The model discussed in this publication is called **Scrumban**, a hybrid version of Kanban and Scrum. This version leverages the features of both models to *Stop Starting* to keep the work in progress at the minimum and *Start Finishing* to reduce the end-to-end lead time. This publication describes **five steps** to implement Scrumban in any Software Maintenance project.

There are multiple versions of Kanban + Scrum already in practice in many organizations. Most have adopted Kanban practices in Scrum to improve flow efficiency and reduce waste. The Scrumban version in this publication discusses the use of Kanban + Scrum in the **Software Maintenance context**, helping work requests that require a Just in Time (JIT) processing model to address the complexities of Software Maintenance.

This publication is based on the author's experience of working with Information Technology (IT) Application Software development and maintenance teams. It shares the basics of Scrumban for teams interested in experimenting and finding their own way of working through challenges. This publication will give insights that allow you to decide whether Scrumban is right for your team and organization, what it takes to implement it, and what to expect from it.

Who this book is for

This book is primarily written for anyone working on Software Maintenance projects - project managers, team leads, process coaches, technology analysts, designers, programmers, testers, and other change agents of the software engineering process groups.

Just to make it simple, if your answer is "yes" to one or more of the following questions, then this book is for you:

1. Is your Software Maintenance and Support team always working on high priority work items?
2. Are there work items which must be delivered on time without being impacted by unplanned and emergency work items?

3. Does your team miss or postpone release dates more often than usual?

How this book is organized

This book is divided into three main parts: **Problem, Solution, and Implementation.** Each part is further divided into several chapters.

Part I – The Problem section describes the needs and complexities of Software Maintenance. What makes Software Maintenance different from Software Development? What are the characteristics that make it complex? This section concludes with a discussion of the changing needs and complexities of Software Maintenance.

Part II – The Solution section describes the execution models currently in practice for Software Maintenance – Traditional Waterfall and Scrum. It also discusses combining Agile and Lean practices to address the needs of Software Maintenance. Lastly, this section develops the most suitable framework for addressing the challenges described earlier.

Part III – The Implementation section describes the five steps needed to implement Scrumban in Software Maintenance. Though it may not serve as a cookbook, this section helps in setting the direction for teams to define their own version of the Scrumban method to **Stop Starting and Start Finishing.**

New to Scrum or Kanban?

If you are new to Scrum or Kanban, do not worry. This book provides a quick refresher on these models in Section 2 – The Solution. For additional reading, I strongly recommend **David J Anderson's Kanban: Successful Evolutionary Change for Your Technology Business**. This book inspired me in many ways to conceptualize and experiment with Scrumban model for Software Maintenance.

Disclaimer

The purpose of this book is to provide a point of view and a perspective to those providing guidance in implementing Scrumban. However, this will not serve as an instructional manual in any way, shape, or form. As discussed earlier, there are many variations of Kanban + Scrum in practice, this is one of the many known variations of the Scrum + Kanban.

The Problem

Chapter 1

One bloody thing after another

"The secret of crisis management is not good vs bad, it's preventing the bad from getting worse." – Andy Gilman

It was early fall season, and like any other work day morning, I arrived at my work place a little later than usual. I walked past security towards the giant elevators that led to the spacious lobby of one of the tallest buildings in downtown Chicago. When I reached my desk, I saw my colleague Sam staring at his web browser, which was loading CNN web site. I could sense frustration in his morning "what's up" nod. Every morning, he has to check the news headlines before he does any work. He can't start his work without this ritual. This means that on working days, I don't have to look at the news headlines. I get a personalized news bulletin from Sam on all the breaking news across the globe.

I logged in to my desktop and opened my email inbox for anything that needed my immediate attention. There were few such emails that day. Even as I glanced through to see what needed to be added to my schedule, I could hear Sam's frustrated grunts in the background. Something must be really wrong with the Internet speed, I thought to myself. Then I saw a major escalation email from one of our clients about an issue with a software change we had recently delivered. I started doing some quick planning to take care of the escalation without impacting existing work that the team has to deliver for the next release. That was when I heard Sam exclaim "DUDE!" I instantly knew that something was really wrong. I routinely hear different versions of that word from Sam and I can tell how bad it is from his tone. I turned to see him staring at the partially loaded CNN page. There it was. The image of a plane crashing into the World Trade Center North Tower. Dense smoke was billowing out of the building. The web page had no content except for this one picture. The rest of the page was still loading. I was stunned, I could not believe what I was seeing.

I walked few steps towards Sam's monitor to see it up close. My mobile phone began buzzing in my pocket, and I answered it automatically while I was still gazing at the screen with CNN page still struggling to load. On the phone, I could hear Conrad, our Server Support Engineer at the data center, speaking agitatedly, "Two of our print servers aren't responding." I didn't realize that I was actually looking at the answer to Conrad's problem. As I stared at the picture for a few seconds, a loud "Hello?" from Conrad brought me back to my senses. I told him, "I know which ones." I knew that our client has an office in the World Trade Center. Before he could answer, I asked him, "Are they New York office print servers?" Before Conrad could confirm, I heard alarms going off in our building. Security personnel were waving at us to exit the building. An emergency evacuation had been ordered as a safety precaution.

The rest of the day was one bloody thing after another. The second plane hit the South Tower, and both towers eventually collapsed. The deadliest visuals I had ever seen. On the work front, I got an emergency request on the Software Maintenance work request, which we delivered earlier. We had to find a way to connect to our Data Center to deliver the fix, and the next day was filled with root cause analysis of those issues, and finding fix into testing and production without impacting other important projects that we are working on. But to deliver this emergency request, we had to stop all the work we were doing and start working on the new emergency request.

In a surreal way, my work situation seemed to parallel the 9/11 situation. The analogy is apt on a smaller scale, because a Software Maintenance and Support team's day is generally "one bloody thing after another." Software Maintenance teams are always in the "fire-fighting" mode, stopping everything on-hand for another crisis, moving from one fire to another, living for the moment, forming SWAT teams, living out of situation rooms, and at the end of the day reaching home exhausted with only one hope that tomorrow will be a better day.

Invariably, most days start and end on the same note – not one less not one more. It is evident that Software Maintenance and Support phase is the most critical phase in the software lifecycle, but it is not given enough importance when compared to Software Development in terms of investments in implementing processes, tools and training. The execution models are inherited from Software Development, as are tools, practices, standards, metrics, and measurements. Over the years, the Software industry has matured with the evolution of many new platforms, process frameworks, and tools.

At the same time, the complexity of software has also seen a manifold increase. The popular belief is that, despite chaotic circumstances and complex scenarios, Software Maintenance teams with their shining armor of platforms, tools, and frameworks are capable of delivering work in a reasonable timeframe.

Curious case of delayed requests

But seriously, with all this chaos going around, how do Software Maintenance teams meet any planned deadlines? Are they delivering changes on time? One would assume that the lead time to deliver a change request is within a reasonable timeframe and meets user expectations. The reality is far from this assumption and most certainly far from the expectations of the end users. Surprised?

A typical maintenance request of 5 days' effort, on average, takes more than 180 days to get into production. Before you scream, "180 days? That's unbelievable!" let me walk you through the maze of activities and wait periods in the typical lifecycle of a maintenance request that will justify this high number. Once the Software Maintenance work request is raised by a user, it is reasonable to expect it to get processed in 2 or 3 weeks, or at most 6 weeks.

However, the work request sets sail on a long uncharted journey: first, it sits in a queue waiting for impact analysis and estimation by the technical team; then, it goes through a prioritization process that typically happens once a month; after that, it sits in a queue waiting for the build. If luck holds, there's only build time. But it might get dropped or deferred depending on the team's other priorities. After the build completion, there's more waiting as it goes through functional testing, system testing, user acceptance testing, and "let's pray for the availability of the environments and testing team's bandwidth" scenarios. There is also the possibility of a change in the requirement or even a defect – this leads to rework, repeating the cycle all over again. Finally, it reaches packaging and deployment, and a final round of waiting for the next deployment window into the production environment.

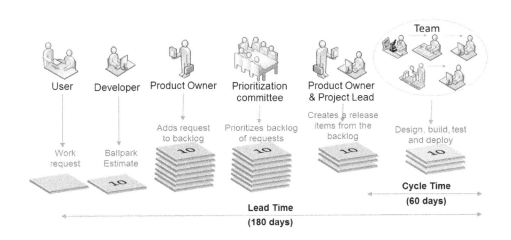

Illustration of Lead Time

How rare are these deployment windows? Well, it might take weeks before one can get a deployment window to move the changes into production. After all this starting, stopping, and waiting, it finally gets delivered to the user. Meanwhile, several weeks, sometimes several months, have passed.

Need #1: Need to reduce the end to end lead time

In this scenario, 180 days could be considered a justifiable period in which to circle back to the user on a typical software change request. This, in spite of having the best in class tools, people, and processes. In fact, in the above scenario, the team would have met all the SLAs, schedule adherence, effort estimates, other service management, and software engineering metrics. Ironic, isn't it? And what about the satisfaction levels among users? It looks like we met the timelines if you start the clock when the team picked up work and stop the clock when the change is delivered to user acceptance testing. So conveniently, organizations measure the cycle time, but measuring end-to-end lead time will give us the real picture of the actual time delay that the user experiences. There is a greater need to focus more on the end-to-end lead time, and less on cycle time reductions and other productivity improvements. Thus, the first need is the "Need to reduce the end-to-end lead time."

Six blind men and the elephant

I want to tell you a story of six blind men and the elephant. And it's not the story you think it is. There were six blind men in a software team. One day, they all went to the zoo to learn about an elephant. However, in this story they did not go to see the elephant together – they went one after another. Our six blind men are called Mr. Business Analyst, Mr. Technical Architect, Mr. Designer, Mr. Programmer, Mr. Reviewer, and Mr. Tester. You can probably imagine the rest of the story. Nothing makes sense if the delivered software does not meet the user's requirements. But why is it so hard to deliver what the business users want?

The question is - business users may know what they want, but are they 100% clear about what they need? The answer is – no. Business' vision of any software feature evolves over a period of time. There is a fundamental difference between want and need. If the want is the starting point of the requirements definition, there is no guarantee that you end up with what user actually need. The actual business requirement of any software feature or change evolves over a period of time, it takes time to fully develop any requirement and bring it to a level for the team to develop.

In this fast-moving world, requirements do not get enough time to evolve. Finalizing the requirements is an iterative process: we must keep at it till we get it right. Agile has seen great success for this reason that all the stakeholders work together in an iterative cycle to build the software feature or a software change. Building software is engineering, but **deciding what software should do is beyond engineering**. In fact, expecting business to give well–documented requirements is next to impossible.

In typical Software Development and Maintenance scenario, it is assumed that business will lay out the requirements up front and the software teams will only go back to business for clarifications to refine their understanding of the requirement. After which they go on a cascade of phases to develop it, with limited exposure to business users regarding the work-in-progress software items during build phases. One fine day, the changed software is released to the business users to validate their requirements, and in a majority of cases, end-user expectations are not met.

Need #2: Need to meet the user requirements

The above scenario is more prevalent in Software Maintenance than in Software Development. With the former, the requirements are seldom documented in detail; there are few "back and forth" discussions on the requirements due to time constraints; prototyping is a rare practice; and hence this ends up as the classic blind men and the elephant story. What gets delivered is a synthesized version of what each of our blind men perceived as the elephant. So, the second need is "Need to meet the end user requirements."

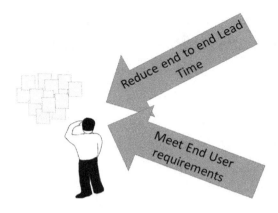

Software Maintenance – Two basic needs

These two needs are basic. The daunting question is: **What makes Software Maintenance so complex that meeting these needs proves to be complex for teams?**

***

Chapter 2

It's like a box of chocolates

"My momma always said, life is like a box of chocolates. You never know what you're gonna get." – Forrest Gump

The above quote perfectly describes Software Maintenance scenario. Software Maintenance is like a box of chocolates; you never know what you are going to get at any moment. The need to measure and reduce the end-to-end lead time and the need to deliver what users want exactly are the two basic needs of Software Maintenance. But what makes it so complex that meeting these basic needs is not as straightforward as it seems? What makes Software Maintenance like a box of chocolates?

Let us back up a bit to understand the typical software lifecycle. Every software goes through various lifecycle stages from conception to the end of life, with various phases - development, evolution, servicing, and end-of-life support. The first major stage that software goes through is the design and development phase. This is when the software gets designed and developed based on the requirements to deliver the intended value.

The Support and Maintenance phases would span across the most active life span of the software, this is when most of the value is delivered. This is when it goes through lot of changes to meet the changing needs of the software. At the end of these stages, it is decided that the software will be replaced by another software, then the changes are restricted to the emergencies changes to keep it operational till it is decommissioned.

This phase is called end of life support, no enhancements are taken up in this phase. After the planned end of life support time period, the software support will be shut down to close out the life cycle.

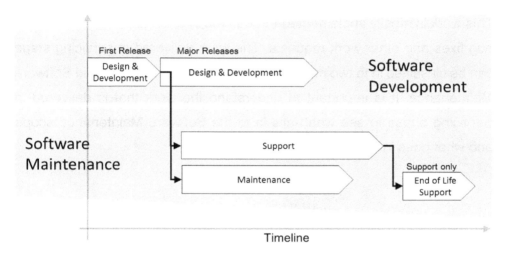

Software Lifecycle stages

The stages that interest the current topic are Servicing and Evolution stages, after the initial Design & Development stage, the software goes through Evolution and Servicing stages in parallel during its prime time of value delivery. During evolution (Design & Development) phase the software goes through functionality related enhancements to meet the changing functional requirements of the software. These are mostly executed as projects or major enhancements, planned and released in annual or semi-annual or quarterly release cycle. This work is considered as development work, but in some cases, it might also be handled by the maintenance teams.

The Maintenance phase and Support phase is when the software is maintained and supported to run with less disruptions and downtime. This could include corrective maintenance to fix the issues, or work requests to make the software adaptive to the changing environment and operating systems, or perfective maintenance to the changing standards of technical and business scenarios and preventive to avoid any possible failure points.

This work is mostly implemented through major and minor enhancements, bug fixes and other work requests. The work delivered in servicing stage can be classified in to two major categories Software Support and Software Maintenance. It is important to understand the work that is delivered in Servicing phase to see what falls in to the Software Maintenance scope and what goes in to the Software Support team.

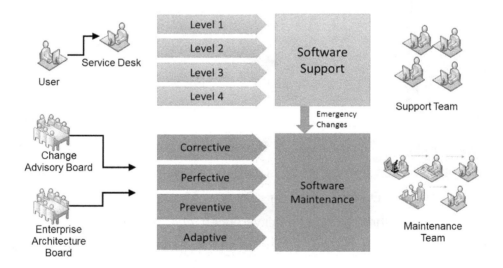

Software Maintenance and Support

Software Support

The Software Support is generally technical support or break/fix services. These services include incident resolution and service request fulfillment, also involves business process monitoring, batch monitoring, troubleshooting, installation assistance, data fixes, and user query assistance. Software support services may include new product installation services, installation of product updates, migrations for major releases of software, and other types of proactive or reactive services. These services are handled in a layered execution model called "Levels", typically there are four levels - Level 1, Level 2, Level 3 and Level 4.

Not all of these levels are classified as Software Maintenance, some part of Level 2 will come in to maintenance team scope, any code changing work of Level 3 and Level 4 is part of maintenance team scope.

Level 1 – First Line of Support

This support level receives inbound requests through channels like phone, Web forms, email, chat, or other means based on the documented agreement with the business and users. This is not part of Maintenance and Support team's scope of work, this is done by Service Desk by a cross functional services.

Level 2 – Second Line of Support

Level 2 team manages incidents raised by the L1 team or as agreed in documented SLA (Service Level Agreement) timelines. L2 technicians follow documented processes and workflows provided by business or L3 or L4 support representatives, vendors, product management, etc. Level 2 team is expected to escalate to the Level 3 team when documentation is insufficient to complete the tasks or do not solve the incident. Some part of the Level 2 work flows in to Maintenance team's scope of work in terms of trouble shooting activities, answering user queries, testing and validation activities, or software installation and setup activities.

Level 3 – Third Line Support

Level 3 technical experts resolve issues that are typically difficult or subtle. L3 engineers participate in management, prioritization, minor enhancements, break fix activities, problem management, stability analysis, etc. most of Level 3 work is Maintenance team's scope of work.

Level 4 – Product and Vendor Support

Level 4 support refers to product or vendor support and often involves vendor product architects, engineers, software developers, hardware designers and the like. When all other levels of support cannot solve a problem, a request is made to this level of support – usually managed by the L3 support technician or through special project/program management resources.

Software Maintenance

The IEEE/EIA 12207 standard for software life cycle processes essentially depicts maintenance as one of the primary life cycle processes, performed after the software delivery to correct faults, to improve performance or other attributes, or to adapt the software to newer environments and business situations. The objective is to modify the existing software product while preserving its integrity.

Software Maintenance can be classified into four types:

1. Adaptive Maintenance – modifying the system to cope with changes in the software environment

2. Perfective Maintenance – implementing new or changed user requirements, which are functional enhancements to the software

3. Corrective Maintenance – diagnosing and fixing errors, possibly defects found by users

4. Preventive Maintenance – increasing software maintainability or reliability to prevent problems in the future

The Software Maintenance and Software Support work requests involve changes to software or its environment varying in scope and size, ranging from a few hours of effort to as large as thousands of hours. Each of these requests involve different sets of activities to fulfill, they come with different priorities and complexities, and they demand different skill sets to complete the job. All the change requests carry certain level of impact and risk associated with them; any malfunction could potentially bring down a running business system to a grinding halt.

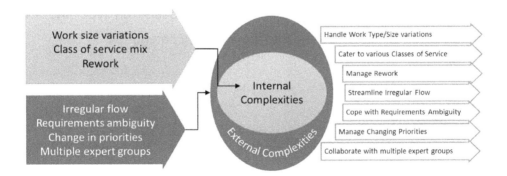

Complexities of Software Maintenance

Every change carries certain amount of impact and risk associated with it; there are many variables which dictate the outcomes. These variables can be categorized into two types – internal and external complexities. For instance, one internal complexity factor could be work size variation. This complexity makes the execution diversified (large enhancement to a simple code fix). On the other hand, the external complexity factors could be requirements ambiguity or the change of priorities of the work request.

Before we jump into finding solution to address these complexities, it is very essential to understand these two types of complexities, which make software maintenance execution uniquely challenging.

Internal Complexities

The internal complexities in Software Maintenance are a set of factors related to the nature of the work, or factors related to the team or factors within the control of the team.

Work Type /Size variations

Software Maintenance work can be classified based on type and size. Broadly, they can be classified into the following categories:

- Enhancements
- Bug fixes
- Service Requests
- Data fixes
- User queries or analysis requests
- Testing requests
- Text or cosmetic changes

Although these different types of work requests are considered as Software Maintenance and Support work requests, each type demands different skill sets, different practices and procedures, different validations and reviews, and different abridged or extended versions of life cycle phases. This variability of work drastically impacts the efficiency of the team members as they have to switch contexts frequently.

The size of the requests also vary drastically where one request would take few hours of effort and another would take hundreds of hours to complete. This size variance demands the teams with multiple skill sets, switching between execution models depending on the size of the request; because smaller work requests may need lighter version of a change request life cycle while larger work requests may need more extensive life cycle phases.

Class of service mix

The Software Maintenance work requests come with various combinations of priorities. These priorities demand different types of service levels, mostly aligned with the urgency and delivery timelines. One such class of service is emergency type; these requests need immediate remediation and could potentially stop all other work requests, and take up most of the available resources.

Another service class is essential work requests, but may not be of an emergency type; such requests could add significant value to the software if implemented. There are other service class work requests, which are date sensitive and the impact of not implementing such requests by a given date is very high. And there is always a class of service work requests, which could be compromised when there is an emergency work request to be serviced. These are requests related to "good to have" features of the software, but would not significantly impact the functionality of the software.

Unlike a development team, maintenance team has to juggle with the diverse class of services and constantly move resources around to meet the expectations. The planning must be Just-in-Time (JIT) or a combination of JIT with conventional planning models. At any point, the team cannot accurately predict the volume of work that flows-in, particularly volumes for each of these classes of service. If emergency class work requests are flowing in frequently, the lowest priority work request would never get done.

The team must adopt a model that could handle variations in the volume of work across all these classes of service without impacting the flow of the work, honoring the priorities of the work requests.

Rework

The rework due to defects reported on the work already delivered to System Testing or User Acceptance Testing generally fall into the high priority category as the testers would be waiting to retest the broken piece of code.

The team has to stop everything on hand to fix these defects, which results in stopping and starting. Switching contexts frequently impacts team's productivity the most. For a programmer, it becomes even more difficult when the defect logged is on a piece of work that was delivered weeks or months ago; getting back into the context makes it even more difficult, making the process inefficient and ineffective.

External Complexities

The external complexity factors of Software Maintenance are a set of factors that are beyond the control of the team. These factors are influenced by the business, environment or organization related. The team is mostly on the receiving end, but these factors heavily influence the outcomes of the team.

Irregular flow

The rate at which the work requests come into the maintenance team's queue is subjected to good amount of fluctuations as it depends on various other external influences. One such influence is that whenever a new version of the software is released, a steady flow of change requests, defect fixes, user queries, and data fix requests would pour in to team's queue. Sometimes, market conditions could also influence the inflow, in peak business seasons, or at a peak time of the year, month, week, or day. Increase in business activities influences work that flows into the maintenance team's queue. At times, it is very hard to predict these irregularities in the flow which makes planning and prioritization a tough nut to crack.

Requirements ambiguity

Typically, business raises a software change request, mostly a one liner description of the change; anything above and beyond means you are having a lucky day. Even if you get clear requirements in the first place, the requirements keep changing, and sometimes even during the integration testing phase.

The traditional waterfall models are designed for product development scenario, where the requirements are frozen to a large extent, and most probably signed off by business analysts or user representatives. But in custom built business applications scenario, the requirement definition is not 100% complete by the end of the requirement phase. This situation leads to lot of ambiguity, and the requirements keep evolving during the software lifecycle, making it a moving target for the team.

Change in priorities (business Vs technical team)

This is one of a very common conflict of interests between business teams and technical teams. Both have their own priorities, business needs to push software changes that help the organization increase revenues or reduce costs or increase the customer satisfaction. The technical teams want software changes that increase the stability of the software or bring it to current versions of technology or increase the security or performance.

Both are important from their own perspectives, business would normally focus on running the business, supporting the growth and cost reductions, and technical team would focus on improving the stability or mitigating other technological risks, improving the resilience of the software and the hosted environment. Many a times, these priorities clash and cause confusion for the Software Maintenance teams and disrupt the rhythm. In the end, the priorities of the business take precedence, which results in stopping and starting of the work to make way for emergency changes. This results in to a nightmare to keep up with the schedules and plans, increasing the lead time for most of the changes which are in-progress or ready to be worked on.

Multiple expert groups

Software complexity grows with its age. Software Maintenance and evolution of systems was first addressed by Meir M. Lehman in 1969. Over a period of twenty years, his research led to the formulation of eight Lehman's Laws. The second Lehman's law states that "Increasing Complexity: As a program is evolved its complexity increases unless work is done to maintain or reduce it," makes it clear that as the software evolves, it grows more complex unless some action is taken to reduce this complexity.

There are internal benchmarking techniques to compare different internal maintenance organizations. IEEE1219–98 suggests measurements that are more specific to Software Maintenance measurement programs. It includes a number of measures for each of the four sub–characteristics of maintainability:

- Analyzability: Measures of the maintainer's effort or resources expended in trying to diagnose deficiencies or causes of failure.
- Changeability: Measures of the maintainer's effort associated with implementing a specified modification.
- Stability: Measures of the unexpected behavior of software, including that encountered during testing.
- Testability: Measures of the maintainer's and users' effort in trying to test the modified software.

As more updates are implemented over a period, vital measurements mentioned above deteriorate. This deterioration of vital measurements makes Software Maintenance the most complex activity. It makes it very difficult to manage Software Maintenance holistically with a single cross functional team. Certain parts of software can only be worked by specialized groups' support, or certain specialized functions can only be carried out by experts in those functions viz. functional testing, performance testing, writing database queries or stored procedures.

Today, DevOps teams are also coming in to picture to be part of the core team to ensure a smooth and faster deployments in to production environment. DevOps will be an additional expert group to be part of the team. But, it is impractical to have experts from all these specialized groups to be present in the team, which results in complex hand-offs increasing the lead time of the work request.

These are the basic needs to be met and required abilities for the teams to execute Software Maintenance efficiently.

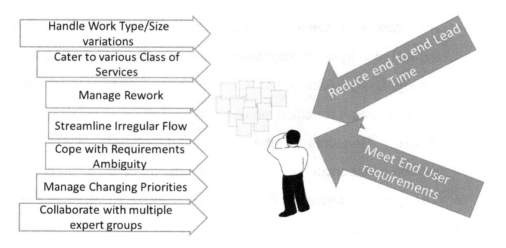

Software Maintenance Complexities

Traditionally, the execution models adopted by the Software Maintenance teams are all the same models which are designed for Software Development. Although it is perfectly reasonable to assume Software Maintenance is the same as Software Development on a smaller scale, as we have seen it is uniquely different from the nature of work and execution perspective. The work types, work size variations, workflow, required skills, and work stages are all different in Software Maintenance, but the execution models adopted are not tailor made for Software Maintenance to address these differences.

The execution models that are in practice are primarily devised for Software Development work, and passed on to the maintenance teams with an assumption that the work is similar. This mismatch in the execution models is making Software Maintenance inefficient and ineffective.

***

Chapter 3

Square peg in a round hole

"I suppose it is tempting, if the only tool you have is a hammer, to treat everything as if it were a nail." – Abraham Maslow

The execution model adopted to deliver Software Maintenance plays a crucial role in achieving delivery excellence. Ironically, Software Development is perceived as the main stream, and Software Maintenance is always subjected to forced-inheritance from the former when it comes to adopting execution models. All the models were primarily designed keeping Software Development in mind, and Software Maintenance teams just inherit these models with an assumption that if it works for development, it will work for maintenance. The point is that the assembly line model works well for manufacturing cars, but not for repairing cars. There is a clear understanding that these two areas are very different given the nature of work, size variations, work flow stages, and skill requirements. It is a well-known fact that the current models in practice for Software Maintenance are good but not the most optimal, like a square peg in a round hole.

Although there are many models, the two most important and widely followed are: the traditional Waterfall model and the Scrum model. Both of these models have advantages and disadvantages, but the fitment must be discussed within the Software Maintenance context. In no way it is deliberated that these models are totally unfit for software management; the models are only subjected to a comparison to see the relevance of these models in the current scenario, considering the complexities and the needs of Software Maintenance.

Waterfall model

Why is a traditional Waterfall model not suitable for Software Maintenance? This question has been beaten to death by many publications, and most of these arguments are true and based on decades of experience. Much like manufacturing assembly line, the Waterfall model is suitable for a sequential execution process. It assumes that every work request goes through each of the five stages (requirements analysis, design, build, testing, and implementation), developers move the software changes from one stage to the next stage sequentially. Once a phase has been completed, developers cannot go back to a previous phase – not without repeating the other phases that follow the previous step. Any change would trigger unplanned iterations, and puts the delivery timelines at risk. That makes the name Waterfall so apt to this model.

It is literally a waterfall, and there is no easy way for any work item to go back up the fall for any reason. Hence, extensive plans must be set in the beginning and must be followed through carefully to avoid any changes that would trigger a revisit to previous phases. Yet even with meticulous planning, there is always the need for a work item to go back up the waterfall, which results in the model's failure to deliver the work on time and within the estimated effort.

It is common knowledge that this model works well when the requirements are clear, workflow is streamlined, and priorities are not changed.

- Once a stage has been completed, developers cannot go back to a previous stage and make changes. Going back would trigger another iteration impacting the actual effort and slipping the delivery dates.

- The Waterfall model relies heavily on initial requirements. But if these requirements are not complete, there is no scope for the requirements evolving during the design phase.

- Any change to the requirements triggers a new iteration. The project has to restart, repeating each phase (requirement analysis, design, building, and testing).

- Validation or testing is done at the end. There is limited opportunity to change the functionality of the software. Users end up receiving something that does not meet their needs.

- The plan doesn't take into account a client's evolving needs. If the client realizes that they need more than they initially thought, and demand change, the project will come in late and impact the budget.

When you should use the Waterfall model?

When the requirements are clear and well documented. When there is very limited chance for change in the requirements (even if there is, it should be within the limits of contingency). When it is not emergency work and can wait its turn to execute. When the business priorities are not changed frequently.

Quick dipstick check

Discussed below are the needs and abilities required for Software Maintenance, and whether the Waterfall model possesses these abilities and meets the needs or not.

Ability to handle Work Type/ Size variations

Irrespective of type or size variations, every request has to go through the same set of lifecycle phases, making it an overhead for small sized or non-software change requests.

Ability to cater to various Classes of Service

There is no special handling for emergency requests or fixed date requests. Every request has to go through the same queue, which makes it inefficient.

Ability to manage Rework

The effort to rework is estimated as a contingency in the initial estimates, which makes this model inflate the estimates; on the other extreme, the estimates may fall short and impact the delivery timelines.

Ability to streamline Irregular Flow

The Waterfall model is not designed to handle workflow fluctuations; it is designed to handle well defined scope of work with limited or no fluctuations in the inflow.

Ability to cope with Requirements ambiguity

There is very little leeway for requirement ambiguity, but not a lot. This model assumes that the requirements are frozen to start the lifecycle.

Ability to manage Changing Priorities

Once the scope is prioritized and fixed, changing the priorities after that would result in waste of effort and might impact the timelines when including the work requests according to the changed priorities.

Ability to collaborate with multiple expert groups

Assumes that the core team consists of all the expertise, which is not very practical when it comes to Software Maintenance.

Reduce the end to end cycle time

The Waterfall model does not provide an end to end cycle view, making it hard to explore any opportunities to reduce the lead time. There is no control over how long a Software Maintenance change takes from the time it is raised to the time it gets delivered.

To meet the end user requirements

In the Waterfall model, the business users won't get a preview of the changes to the software during the build cycles. They will only get to see the final deliverable at the end. This makes the probability of not meeting the user requirements very high.

Scrum Model

Scrum evolved as a "solution" to address the disadvantages of the Waterfall model. Instead of a sequential process, Scrum follows an incremental approach. Scrum is among the widely used Agile methodology for Software Development. This model is also used for Software Maintenance by many organizations.

The team starts off with a simplistic project design, and then begins to work on small modules. The scope of work of these modules is revisited in weekly or monthly sprints, and at the end of each sprint, project priorities are evaluated and tests are run. These sprints allow for bugs to be discovered, and customer feedback to be incorporated into the design before the next sprint is started. The process, with its lack of initial design and steps, is often criticized for its collaborative nature that focuses on principles rather than the process.

Disadvantages of the Scrum model

Scrum is primarily designed for Software Development, and not for Software Maintenance. In Software Maintenance, the work is a steady flow and not a pool of work to be managed and executed. Once a sprint is in progress, there is no possibility of dropping or adding work in the middle of the sprint.

Release cycles are on a fixed frequency. It is not flexible enough to deliver higher priority items before the scheduled sprint delivery date. Anything not part of the current sprint has to wait for the next sprint.

When you should use Scrum?

When the requirements are not clear or there is a scope for change in the requirements or there is no clear picture of the final product. Scrum demands cross-functional and multi-skilled developers who are adaptable and are able to think independently. It is relevant when the product is intended for an industry with rapidly changing requirements.

How does Scrum model measure up?

Discussed below are the needs and abilities required for Software Maintenance and whether the current model has these abilities and meets the needs or not.

Ability to handle Work Type/ Size variations

Every work item has to be split into smaller story points. This may not be possible with all the work items; some have to be delivered as one piece, and some are very small and therefore cannot be brought to a standard sized story.

Ability to cater to various Classes of Service

Everything is bundled into the sprints; if there is an emergency request to be serviced, it can only be delivered as part of one of the future sprints.

Ability to manage rework

The rework within the limits can be handled in the same sprint, if not added to the backlog to get it into one of the future sprints.

Ability to streamline Irregular Flow

The Scrum model works well with a pile of work to be delivered in regular intervals; it is not very effective in a scenario where the work flows in an irregular fashion. In effect, it has only one cadence and is boxed into an iteration. Once the sprint back log is prioritized, that is the only work in progress; rest of the work will have to wait for the next sprint, irrespective of the flow fluctuations.

Ability to cope with requirements ambiguity

Scrum has the ability to handle requirement ambiguity during grooming and planning, and the fine tuning of the requirements happens during the sprint execution.

Ability to manage changing priorities

The change in priorities of the backlog items is possible at any time, but the work that is already in the sprint, priority cannot be changed. Any high priority request has to wait for the next iteration, and there is no way it can be included in the current sprint.

Ability to collaborate with multiple expert groups

The Scrum model is designed for a cross functional team; time sharing expert groups are done in exceptional cases, but not advisable. It does not work in situations where the expertise falls outside the Scrum team.

Reduce the end to end cycle time

The Scrum model provides an end to end cycle view to a certain extent on the work that is in the backlog (mostly known defects and enhancements), making it easy to explore any opportunities to reduce the cycle time. But the work that comes in under an emergency makes the reduction of end to end cycle time a challenge.

Meet the end user requirements

In the Scrum model, the business user gets a preview of the software changes. This particular need is met to a large extent by adopting a Scrum model.

The above two models, Waterfall and Scrum, could be serving the purpose of Software Maintenance teams, but they are definitely square pegs in round holes. All the seven abilities and two basic needs are not met. It leaves us with a need to adopt a model that has the best features from all the models to address the complexities and needs of Software Maintenance.

***

Chapter 4

The problem is not knowing the problem

"If I had one hour to save the world, I would spend fifty-five minutes defining the problem and only five minutes finding the solution." - Albert Einstein

The real problem is not knowing the problem; once you know what the problem is, you are very close to finding a solution. The definition of the problem will be the focal point of all your problem-solving efforts. It makes a lot of sense to devote as much attention as possible in defining the problem, and the solution will follow automatically. What usually happens is that as soon as we have a problem to work on, we are so eager to get to a solution that we neglect spending any time refining the problem definition. What most of us do not realize and what supposedly Einstein might have been alluding to, is that the quality of the solutions we come up with will be in direct proportion to the quality of the problem definition.

Software Maintenance is different

It was discussed extensively in the previous chapters of this book that the type of work, size variations, work flow stages, and required skills are all different in Software Maintenance. While complexities are pinning us down and the basic needs are staring straight into our eyes, the models adopted are not tailor made for Software Maintenance. The models currently adopted are primarily devised for Software Development teams, and are passed on to the maintenance teams who inherited these models with some minor adjustments. It is time to look at Software Maintenance as a separate domain and design models to suit the requirements.

All the complexities discussed so far result in the team members stopping work requests which are currently in progress and starting new ones with higher priority. These interruptions result in work getting piled up, and leading to longer lead times.

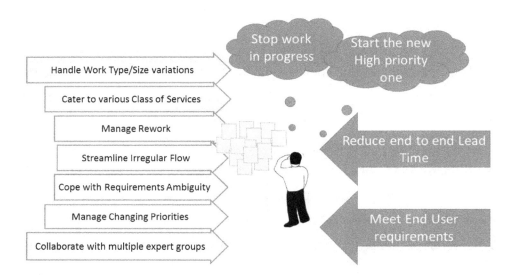

Software Maintenance dilemma

The stopping and starting of work requests result in team members switching context from one request to another, very often leads to loss of productivity and increased error rates. In summary, stopping and starting slows down the teams, increasing the average Lead Time to deliver the work and impacting the efficiency of teams significantly.

Business Agility

Business Agility enables organizations to keep pace with changing market conditions, capitalize on emergent business opportunities, and adopt new business models to reduce costs or increase revenues. From the software point of view, there are three blocks which play an important role in increasing or decreasing the Business Agility of any organization. These three blocks are Demand, Develop and Deploy.

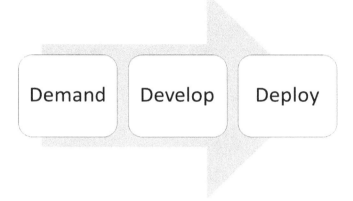

Three blocks of Business Agility

Demand block is where the business changes are generated, Develop is where the business changes are designed and developed, and the Deploy block is where the changes will be deployed in to production. Any block not matching the throughput of the other blocks would make the entire flow slower and results in decrease in throughput.

Few years ago, business models used to seldom change, and when there are changes the Develop and Deploy blocks used to get enough time to deliver, or rather the timelines were acceptable to the organizations. Today, Demand part is becoming more and more dynamic, business models are changing at a rapid pace, forcing the Develop and Deploy to increase their agility to stay abreast with the pace of Demand block.

Demand – Business functionality is changing often and requirements are ever evolving

As the business is constantly changing, as a result triggering changes in business models and underlying functions, processes, policies and procedures. These business changes reflect in the software and technology layers to enable organization to conduct business. The days of long requirement gathering phases are gone. Now, business wants to kick start the build phase before even documenting the requirements. The requirement gathering, analysis, design, coding, testing, and user acceptance phases are not executed in a sequence anymore. Rather, they are done in parallel to make the whole process agile. Since the requirements are ever evolving in today's scenario, the execution model should be able to address this challenge to make Software Maintenance efficient. The models that are not agile and lean are getting extinct, the only models that survive are the ones which can handle this ever changing requirements scenario.

Deploy – Need for agility and high quality

To match the speed of the business demands of today's scenario, organizations are adopting newer deployment models. The disjointed approach of separate development team and operations team is diminishing rapidly. DevOps is catching up like wild fire, in few years DevOps will become a prerequisite for Software Development and Maintenance. DevOps is a cultural and professional movement that stresses collaboration, communication and integration between software developers and operations teams. It responds to accelerated demands for high quality software products and services, acknowledges the interdependency of various IT functions, recognizes the need for cultural improvements and leverages Agile, Lean and ITSM and encourages Automation.

DevOps is the combination of philosophies, practices, and tools that increases an organization's ability to deliver goods and services at high velocity: evolving and improving software at a faster pace than organizations traditional software management processes. This speed enables organizations to better serve their customers and compete more effectively in the market.

Develop – Need to match the pace

Demand block is generating the need for software changes faster than ever, and the Deploy block is catching up adopting to DevOps and other agile deployment models, shifting the focus on to Develop block entirely.

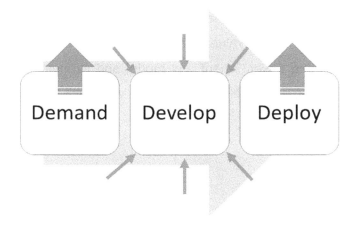

Develop becoming the bottleneck

With Demand and Deploy delivering higher throughput, the software change requests get piled up at Develop block impacting the Business Agility of the organization. The problem is to increase the agility of the Develop block by implementing a new model.

New generation workforce is different

Millennials (also known as the Millennial Generation or Generation Y) are the demographic group following Generation X are the majority of the workforce today. Most researchers use birth years ranging from the early 1980s to 2000 as the Millennial or Generation Y workforce. By 2015, Millennials (ages 18-35) make up 30%-35% of the workforce (70%-75% by 2025).

The basic expectations of Millennials are to work wherever they want, work whenever they want and work on whatever they want. These programmers like their freedom and flexibility. The new generation programmers come with a new set of characteristics, beliefs, paradigms, and work habits. If you expect your team to consist of Millennials and the generation Z then the execution models must make sense to them, every step they take should be logical, and should add value to them or to the work they deliver. These are not programmers who inherit any model and live with it. They adopt models that allow them to deliver high quality work with high productivity in their own way.

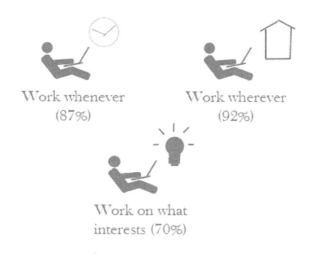

Work whenever
(87%)

Work wherever
(92%)

Work on what
interests (70%)

Needs of Generation Y programmers

The models should allow the new generation programmers to be empowered to pick their work rather than assigning work to them, to be able to work with the end user rather than going through the hierarchy, and to be able to have less restrictions in terms of policies and processes, rather than having only one way to execute work. The success of any model is heavily dependent on the adoption of it wholeheartedly by the Software Maintenance teams.

The traditional models in practice do not provide much-needed freedom and flexibility to the teams and the result of which is quite evident from the success of these models. The crux of the problem lies in the fact that Software Maintenance is different, business needs agility, and the Gen Y programmers demand a new paradigm.

As we all agree, knowing the problem definition makes us focus all our efforts on the right solution, so far we have discussed many aspects of Software Maintenance which brings us close to knowing the problem and leads us to devising a suitable model. A model that is right for Software

Maintenance, a model that meets the basic needs and has all the required capabilities, a model that is suitable for the current and future generations of programmers, and a model that caters to the Lean and Agility demands of the business.

***

The Solution

Chapter 5

Entering the inmost cave

"The cave you fear to enter holds the treasure you seek." - Joseph Campbell

The ability to stop starting and start finishing, the ability to deliver anytime, the ability to handle requirement ambiguity, the ability to collaborate with multiple groups, and the ability to reduce switching contexts is the recipe for a successful model of Software Maintenance. A model that reduces the end to end lead time and a solution that delivers the changes that meet 100% of end user requirements can only be derived from addressing the complexity factors that are working against meeting these basic needs.

By closely examining the symptoms of stopping and starting of the work, one can conclude the inefficiency is caused due to a few work requests that are interruption-prone. These requests impact the other requests that pass through the same channel. But not all the maintenance work is interruption prone, and these work requests can be delivered without any delays in an ideal scenario. However, the same team works on both types of work, and the interruptions caused by some part of the work, impacts the other.

In an ideal situation, we will be able to isolate the work that is interruption-free and use an efficient "Push model" to deliver on this. The other part, which is prone to interruptions, should be handled with a pull model. This arrangement will enable one part of the work to be delivered without interruptions, and the second part of work to be delivered by smartly handling the complexity factors to deliver high flow efficiency. In addition, implementing pull effect in a push model would augment efficiency levels.

Before we go any further on this topic, it is essential to define certain concepts to set the context for our current model. As these terms are defined and understood in various different ways according to specific context, it is a fact that there are already many disagreements on the definition of these models in the Agile and Lean communities. The intention is not to create more confusion but to set the context for this publication.

Push and Pull models

The Push and Pull methods are used to manage the movement of work in the production line. In manufacturing industry, these models are based on the demand and forecast to optimize the inventory levels. What makes them push or pull model is based on how the work is planned, managed and delivered to optimize the inventory or resources.

Push model

The Push model is "Make to Stock" (MTS), this is not based on the actual demand, it is based on forecast. A work order is pushed through various process steps from start to end to deliver a finished product or work order. It does not depend on the demand on the right side, which is the actual order of this product.

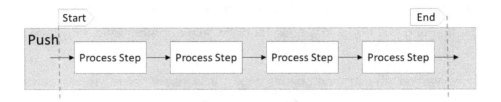

Push model

In software, the traditional models are built around the Push model. The work request, mostly "new feature" or "bug fix", is assigned to a team member. Each member of the team have their own personal queue of tasks and they focus only on items in their personal queue. Some attempt is made to level the queues across the team but as time progresses the queues need to be re-leveled and if they're not re-leveled frequently enough then some people can become starved for work while others are overloaded. Over time it becomes very difficult to predict when any given task might be completed because it depends on both whose queue it is in and what is ahead of it in that queue. While in the work period (sprint or milestone) the question of which stories are done and which are still in progress is really quite non-deterministic. The only thing that can be said with certainty is that when everyone's queues are empty, all the stories are done.

Pull model

The Pull model is "Make to Order" (MTO), this is based on the actual demand. Pull model is based on the demand side such as Just-in-Time (JIT) and CRP (Continuous Replenishment Program) while inventory is kept to a minimum, orders can be fulfilled with short lead times at increased speed.

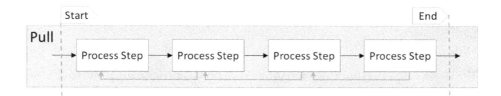

Pull model

Pull models are making their headway in Software Maintenance, though the pull method in Software Maintenance is slightly different from the manufacturing industry definition. The work requests that flow in to the backlog are ordered according to their priority and the time of arrival. The next available team member pulls a work request from the top of the backlog, completes the stage and places it in the "done" bucket for the next stage team member to pull. This goes on till the work request reaches the finish line.

Escalator Vs Elevator

A very good analogy of these Push and Pull models is the symbolic comparison between Escalator and Elevator. The "Push type" can be considered as an escalator. An escalator continues to supply (push) regardless of whether there is actual demand (passenger). In addition, "Push type" corresponds to a model for trains, buses, and airplanes for which supply (push) is based on demand forecast by time period and route. Whereas an elevator starts when a button is pressed even if there is only one passenger, this is a pull type as the service is based on the demand. There may be various forms between "Push type" and "Pull type" depending on inventory forms of materials, work in progress (WIP), and finished items and how to deal with the actual demand in supply chain management.

CONWIP

Constant Work In Progress (CONWIP) is classified as pull and push system. In a Push model, the work order is scheduled and the material is pushed into the production line. In a Pull model, the start of each production line is triggered by the completion of another at the end of production line. CONWIP is a kind of single-stage Kanban system and is also a hybrid push-pull system. While Kanban systems maintain tighter control of system WIP through the individual cards at each workstation, CONWIP systems are easier to implement and adjust, since only one set of system cards is used to manage system WIP. For example, no part is allowed to enter the system without a card (authority). After a finished part is completed at the last workstation, a card is transferred to the first workstation and a new part is pushed into the sequential process route.

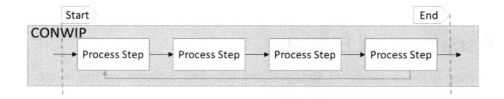

CONWIP model

Putting a constraint on the Work in Progress (WIP) at the entire cycle is CONWIP, but Kanban applies the WIP limit at each work stage. This causes a pull effect without stalling the entire cycle, and forces each stage to pull work and improve the flow.

However, using the CONWIP concept of attaching a card (limited) to work request restricts the number of requests across all the stages, which helps in improving the pull effect further. The push and pull terms originated in logistics and supply chain management, but later Agile and Lean methodologies adopted them in Software Development and Maintenance. In Software Development and Maintenance, Push and Pull models are based on capacity availability to optimize human resources. In addition, implementing CONWIP principles would make this model more efficient.

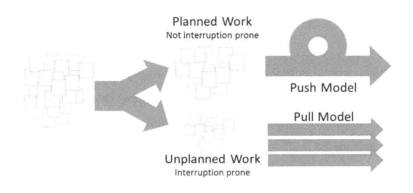

Push and Pull Model

The work that flows into Software Maintenance is of two major categories. The first category of work is software enhancements, mostly planned work, predictable, and less interruption prone.

The second category consists of various types of maintenance work, which are basically non-enhancements – software bug fixes, service requests, data fixes, PTC or cosmetic changes, user queries, analysis requests and testing requests – mostly unplanned work, unpredictable, and more interruption prone. There is a theory that planned work is better handled by a push model and unplanned can be better handled by a pull model. Whether that theory is true or not, it is understood that Software Maintenance has both these categories of work and a combination of push and pull model would definitely help in improving the efficiency.

1. Planned work (Enhancements)

The planned work or software enhancements are mostly a scaled down version of Software Development work. Considering this work as more predictable and less prone to interruptions, the best model to employ for this kind of work is Agile Scrum – supports continuous delivery, has better end to end cycle time, handles the requirement ambiguity, and provides a preview to stakeholders.

Scrum has been successfully implemented by many software practitioners and it definitely needs no introduction. It is the number one widely accepted practice within software projects that follow Agile methods. 60% of Agile teams follow Scrum.

In recent times, applying Kanban principles to the Scrum model proved a good practice to introduce the pull factor to augment the flow efficiency and deliver better predictability. This is called as Scrumban, in its pure form for Software Development. But the Scrumban version that is discussed in this publication is a customized version of Scrumban for Software Maintenance.

2. Unplanned work (Non–Enhancements)

The second category of the work as mentioned above is unplanned work or non-enhancement related work. These are operational requests or activities such as software bug fixes, service requests, data fixes, user queries, analysis requests, and testing requests. This work is less predictable and more prone to interruptions. A pull method is ideal for addressing the challenges posed by continuous flow work. The Kanban model is on the rise in Software Maintenance and Support because of its flexible nature and its focus on flow efficiency.

Kanban is a pull method implemented in the manufacturing industry. In recent times, this was customized to improve the efficiency of Software Development and Maintenance processes. The model is very effective where work flows in, where work requests are smaller, and where work requires the participation of specialist teams.

Scrum and Kanban are viewed as the shining knights of Agile methodology. They reduce the chaos and unpredictability in the Software Development and Maintenance processes. Considering the nature of Software Maintenance that demands Agile and Lean methods, a hybrid version of Scrum + Kanban, called 'Scrumban', started creating quite a stir in recent times. The popularity of this hybrid concept is growing by leaps and bounds, and has an incredible success rate.

For better clarity, let us define these two methods separately before evaluating whether or not a hybrid is an ideal match for Software Maintenance.

What is Scrum?

Scrum is an iterative, incremental process for maintaining software in complex environments to improve agility and predictability. Scrum is focused to split the organization into small, cross-functional as well as self-organizing teams. Also, the time is divided into short, fixed-length iterations. Work is broken into "user stories". Small sets of user stories are estimated and brought into the individual sprint backlog, then built, tested, and made ready for production. The next set of stories is picked up in the next sprint and this process repeats till all the user stories are completed. The number of "user stories" completed in one sprint contributes to velocity.

Agile Scrum manifesto:

- Values the **individual and interactions** over process and tools
- Values **working software** over comprehensive documentation
- Values **customer collaboration** over customer negotiation
- Values **responding to change** over following a plan

"Scrum provides an iterative, incremental process for developing and maintaining software in complex environments"

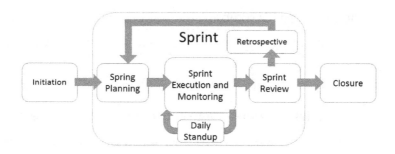

Scrum model

Main features of Scrum:

1. Short sprint iterations
2. Daily stand-ups
3. Demos to stakeholders
4. Retrospectives

Main benefits of Scrum:

1. Accelerate Time to Market
2. Early and continuous user validation
3. Great visibility into project progress
4. Early defect detection and prevention

5. Risk reduction and quality improvements

6. Improved team morale

What is Kanban?

Kanban is a pull method for highly collaborative and self-managed teams to limit work in progress items, and uses visual workflow to improve the flow efficiency and cycle times. Kanban helps the team to visualize the workflow and focus on improving flow efficiency of the work. The work is divided into pieces making it easy to manage. Limiting the work in progress during each workflow state is key to successful implementation. It is a systematic approach when it comes to measure, visualize, and follow up a project work in a system.

"Kanban is for highly collaborative and self-managed teams limiting work in progress items, and visualizing workflows to improve the throughput and cycle time"

Kanban literally means "signboard" or "billboard". It is a scheduling system for lean and just-in-time (JIT) production. Kanban is a system to control the logistical chain from a production point of view, and is not an inventory control system. Kanban was developed by Taiichi Ohno, at Toyota, to find a system to improve and maintain a high level of production. Kanban is one method through which JIT is achieved.

Kanban became an effective tool in support of running a production system as a whole, and it proved to be an excellent way of promoting continuous improvement.

Main features of Kanban:

1. Visualize the workflow: The workflow of knowledge work is inherently invisible. Visualizing the flow of work and making it visible is core to understanding how the work progresses. Without understanding the workflow, making the right changes is harder. A common way to visualize the workflow is to use a card wall with cards and columns. The columns on the card wall represent the different states in the workflow.

2. Limit WIP: Limiting work-in-process implies that a pull system is implemented in certain stages or in all the stages of the workflow. The pull system will act as one of the main stimuli for continuous, incremental, and evolutionary changes to your system.

3. Manage flow: The flow of work through each stage in the workflow should be monitored, measured, and reported. By actively managing the flow, the continuous, incremental and evolutionary changes to the system can be evaluated to assess the positive or negative effects on the system.

Main benefits of Kanban:

1. Bottlenecks become clearly visible in real-time. This leads team members to collaborate and optimize the whole value chain, rather than just their part.

2. Provides a more gradual evolution path from Waterfall to Agile and Lean software management, thereby motivating teams that previously have been unable or unwilling to try Agile methods.

3. Provides a way to engage in agile Software Development and Maintenance without necessarily having to use time-boxed, fixed-commitment iterations such as Scrum sprints. Useful for situations where sprints do not make much sense, such as operations and support teams with a high rate of uncertainty and variability.

Why not implement Scrum and Kanban separately?

Scrum and Kanban models have unique strengths, but also have weaknesses that could constrain Software Maintenance significantly. A hybrid version of these two models could potentially overcome the weaknesses and complement the strengths of each model. But before we conclude that this combination is ideal, and hybrid model is the elixir we are all looking for, one must ask a question: "Why not implement Scrum and Kanban separately?"

It is quite logical to ask this question. These two models seem to be the best in their respective scenarios, though we understand that the two main categories of work demand both push and pull methods. While from a theoretical point of view it makes sense to adopt a hybrid model, it is worthwhile to question it. Why not implement Scrum and Kanban separately? What does this hybrid version bring to the table?

One team, one scope and one model

Firstly, the team is one team, with one scope of work to deliver Software Maintenance and Support. There are various reasons for it to stay as one team, sometime the contracts are written in such a way that they have to be executed as one team, sometimes because of the skill and knowledge reasons it has to be one team. Implementing separate execution models will create confusion even when the boundaries are very well defined. A hybrid model makes it one model for the team to follow. Any synergies from the planning, executing, monitoring, and reporting point of view would augment the benefits of both the models. On the other hand, the work that flows into Software Maintenance is of various types with very distinct characteristics, and demand different execution models to make the team efficient.

The crux of the problem is that all the execution models adopted so far expose the team to the complexities of Software Maintenance work. Implementing Scrum and Kanban as two separate models may reduce the severity of the problem, but will still not resolve the core problem of segregating and channeling the work into the right cadence. Scrumban is a vehicle with two engines working together to address the diverse needs of Software Maintenance with its combined abilities. Hence, a hybrid of Scrum and Kanban must be implemented, instead of implementing them separately.

Scrum needs pull effect

Software Maintenance work demands a push and pull model, as discussed above the planned work is less interruption prone and push model is most suited. Scrum is a push model, but unless we add the pull effect the flow efficiency will not improve to suit the requirements of Software Maintenance scenario.

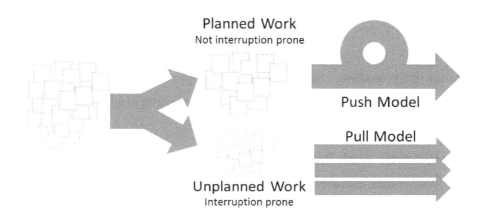

Push and Pull model

How do we add pull factor? It is discussed in a later chapter by introducing the "Doing" and "Done" columns within a stage, and by implementing Work In Progress (WIP) limit. These are Kanban practices that will introduce pull factor to the Scrum to make the flow more efficient.

The more interruption-prone unplanned work is not suited for a push model, but can be managed well with a push & pull model. The pull model will dampen the effect of frequent interruptions to balance the priorities to maximize the throughput. In summary, the hybrid of Scrum and Kanban will address the complexities of Software Maintenance, not their separate implementation.

Why Scrum + Kanban is a perfect combination?

It seems evident that Software Maintenance requires a pull and push model, Scrum and Kanban together forms the push and pull effect, however the best test would be to gauge Scrumban against internal and external complexities, required abilities, and the needs of Software Maintenance work that were discussed earlier in this publication.

Ability to handle Work Type/ Size variations

Scrumban major cadences for Enhancements and Non–Enhancements create a push and pull effect, and Type/Size/Class of work as sub–cadences further add additional pull effect to improve the flow efficiency. This model has a great ability to handle work type/size variations.

Ability to cater to various Classes of Service

Various service classes defined in Scrumban according to the scenario should be able to handle the service class mix of work that flows in for Software Maintenance. This would also enable the team to process some expedite classes to be released anytime. Inherently, Scrumban delivers all classes of services without impacting them by limiting Expedite class services.

Ability to manage Rework

Rework can be classified into two main categories, expedite and non–expedite type. The expedite work items, for example, are bugs that must be fixed as part of the current release; those should be made part of the current sprint or addressed in the prioritized backlog.

The non-expedite work items should be added to the sprint backlog or the backlog items so that they are processed in the consequent releases.

Ability to streamline Irregular Flow

The cadences are designed to handle the irregularities in the flow; cadences and WIP limits are defined and refined according to the flow patterns. These two levers help in handling fluctuations of the work in flow.

Ability to cope with Requirements ambiguity

Scrum and Kanban models address the requirement ambiguity well with their inherent features. Both models have business or users part of the team working closely to resolve requirement ambiguity, and evolve requirements during the lifecycle stages.

Ability to manage Changing Priorities

Scrum is not conducive to change the priorities in the middle of a sprint. In Kanban, if there is an urgent request to implement or an important user story, the team can just assign it to top of the queue. In general, both models have bare minimum work items in the work in progress stage; for Scrum, it is mostly the work that is already in the current sprint; for Kanban, the work that is already on the board – Work In Progress items. The rest of the work is anyway waiting in the backlog; therefore, changing priority may be relatively easier with Scrumban compared to other models. Changing the priority of the work requests whose work is already in progress may not be possible on Planned Work cadence, but the work requests on the Unplanned Work cadence can be dropped to backlog and other priority items can be taken up, or another item from a lower service class cadence can be dropped to pick up a high priority item.

Ability to collaborate with multiple expert groups

Kanban has the inherent ability to handle multiple expert groups; hence, the work that involves multiple groups should be passed through the Unplanned Work cadence, and the work that can be carried out by the cross functional team should pass through Planned Work cadence.

Reduce the end to end cycle time

Scrumban model provides an end to end cycle view, making it easy to explore any opportunities to reduce cycle time. Push and Pull methods working in tandem would ensure that the flow efficiency is higher. For example, WIP limit increases the focus on work in progress, which would result in less stopping and starting, and more of finishing the work. Various cadences would help in streamlining the work with different priorities and of different types to get appropriate attention without disrupting the rhythm of the team.

Meet the end user requirements

Increased business or end user involvement in this model decreases the requirement ambiguity, and the delivered work meets the end user requirements completely.

***

Chapter 6

Scrumban - Introduction

"Start by doing what's necessary; then do what's possible; and suddenly you are doing the impossible." - Francis of Assisi

What is Scrumban?

The Scrum model was successful worldwide in terms of adoption and delivered phenomenal value, but many teams and organizations have struggled to implement all of its aspects in Software Maintenance. The challenges could be related to not being able to meet iteration or release level commitments of scope and time including the nature of work not fitting into iterations, inability to deliver emergency changes, failing to work with multiple groups, not responding adequately to the changing priorities, or not being able to handle the requirement ambiguity. If you have faced some of these challenges, and you are looking for ways to improve your Scrum processes, then you should be looking at Scrumban, a hybrid model by applying Kanban principles on Scrum to deliver higher flow efficiency. Kanban compliments Scrum by introducing the pull factor in to the push model. It helps in delivering the work that is more of flow than picking up from a pool of work.

Scrum model is designed to deliver stories or work requests continuously, and Kanban principles dampen the effects of the interruptions on the flow to improve the throughput of the team.

In a nutshell…

Identify various work types and create two or three main cadences to streamline the work that flows through the team. The basis for forming these cadences is whether the nature of work is disruption prone or not. Add an Expedite cadence to enable emergency work items to flow through without impacting rest of the work in progress. Create release cycles aligning with these cadences and deliver predictable amount of work. Introduce pull effect across the stages of the lifecycle to monitor and manage the flow.

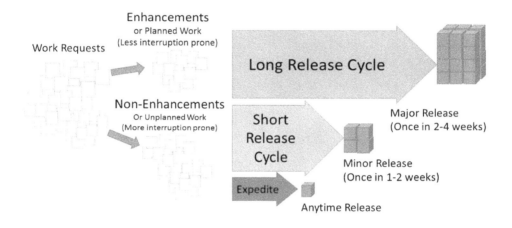

Illustration of Scrumban for Software Maintenance

Practices

All the Scrumban practices are derived from Scrum and Kanban models. However, there are slight variations when adapting these practices to a Software Maintenance scenario. Following sections discuss various practices of Scrumban for you to consider while setting up the model in your scenario.

Visualization

The first and foremost practice is to visualize the work and flow of work. Visualization helps in forming major cadences. The visualization process should be based on the work type in terms of whether or not the work is interruption prone, for enhancements (planned work) and non-enhancements (unplanned work). Once these main cadences are formed, visualize the sub cadences required to further streamline the workflow.

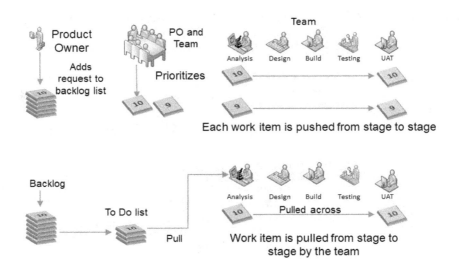

Visualization of work in Push and Pull scenarios

This second level visualization is very crucial in deciding the sub cadences. Under the Planned Work cadence, the sub cadences can be Application group based, technology group based, or could involve some other logical grouping. Under the Unplanned Work cadence, the sub cadences can be class-of-service based, work type based, or work size based. A common way to visualize the workflow is to use a card wall with cards in rows and columns. The columns represent various stages, phases, or steps in the workflow. The rows represent cadences.

Cadence or Bucket size planning

This practice is to primarily arrive at capacity distribution across the cadences. Cadence size or Bucket size planning is done in the initial phases of Scrumban implementation. In this planning, the existing volumes of work flowing into the Software Maintenance team is analyzed to arrive at a cadence or a bucket size for enhancements (planned work) and non-enhancements (unplanned work). It turns out that if X% of effort is reserved for Planned Work, then (100–X) % would be available for the Unplanned Work. For example, when the effort required for planned work is 60% on average, the buckets are formed with 60:40 capacity split between Planned Vs Unplanned Work. The bucket sizes can be refined in the first 2–3 iterations, but should be kept at the same size afterwards to maintain metric accuracy.

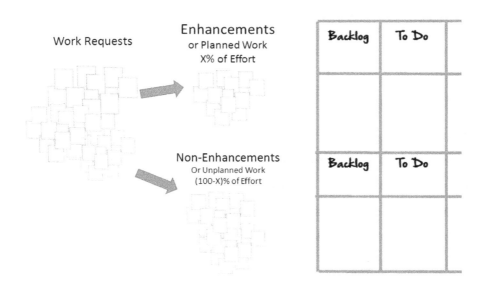

Cadence or Bucket planning

Planned work (enhancements) cadence is run like any Scrum sprint.

Depending on the size, there could be multiple Planned Work cadences running in parallel – Scrums of Scrums. These can be planned as iterations or as a continuous flow with fixed delivery frequency.

Unplanned Work cadence needs further analysis to form sub-cadences based on Work Type or Class of Service or Business Areas or Technologies. This topic is discussed in detail in a later chapter.

On-demand planning

Scrumban triggers on-demand planning based on the number of work requests left in the "To Do" section of the board. When it goes down to a certain number, the planning event is held. This threshold number depends on team velocity and on the time required to plan the next iteration. The work requests planned for the next iteration are added to the "To Do" section of the board.

Pull practice

In Scrumban, the work is not assigned to team members by a Scrumban Master. Each team member chooses the work request or task from the "To Do" section of each stage (analysis, design, coding, testing), pulls the work to the "Doing" section and then starts processing the request. This guarantees a smooth workflow, and work load is equally distributed across team members.

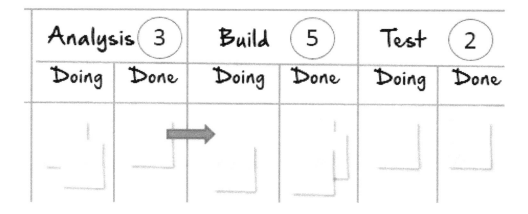

Pull practice

Typically, work is passed through various stages (analysis, design, coding and testing) before it gets delivered as a completed story or work request. Introducing the pull effect across the stages improves the flow and delivers better throughput. This is achieved by applying two practices of Kanban over Scrum.

Adding "Doing" and "Done" columns

Adding "Doing" and "Done" columns under each work flow stage would enable the team to place the work in "Done" column after the work in that phase is complete, and once a team members gets free would pick up story or work item from the "Done" column and move it in to the "Doing" column of the next stage.

Limit WIP

Limiting work-in-process implies that a pull system is implemented in parts or all through the workflow. The pull system will act as one of the main stimuli for continuous, incremental, and evolutionary changes to your system. The WIP limit at each stage or state in the workflow is limited, and new work is "pulled" into the new information discovery activity when there is available capacity within the local WIP limit. Setting up a WIP limit is mandatory on all cadences and all stages except the ones in the beginning and end, such as Back Log, To Do and Done columns. Setting a Work In Progress (WIP) limit at stage level will reduce work getting piled up in any one stage. Because work piling up means increased lead time, it leads to constrained flow which impacts the overall team efficiency.

Backlog	To Do	Build	Test	UAT	Deploy	Done
	5	2	2	∞	∞	

Limiting Work in Progress

Shifting contexts is very unproductive. A team member should be working on no more than one task at a time. To make sure this rule is followed a WIP (work in progress) limit is implemented. This limit is visually represented at the top of the stage on the board. This means that only that amount of work requests or tasks can be in the corresponding column at any time. WIP limit is usually equal to the number of people working in that stage, but could be expanded based on the team and type of work.

Iterations

It is not mandatory to have the iterations. Some Scrumban implementations have iterations and some don't. The iterations in Scrumban are on the Planned Work cadence. The iterations are prescribed to be short in duration, which enables the team to be flexible to the change in priorities. The ideal length of an iteration depends on the function of the project, it is recommended to have iteration length be a maximum of four weeks and a minimum of one week, but two weeks is ideal iteration length. It is also dependent on the release cycle of your organization.

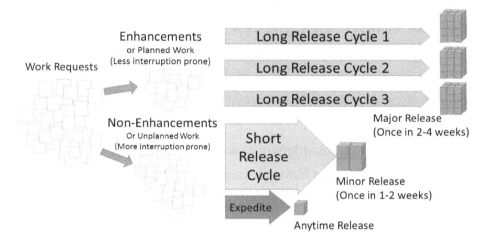

Iterations in Scrumban

It is a common scenario to have more than one iteration, and typically, the team size not exceeding 9 people. You may stretch the team size to 14 or 15 people, but anything beyond, it is better to form multiple teams. For instance, if the volume of work in the planned cadence is more than one team's capacity (9 people), there is a need to form multiple teams delivering in parallel releases. These teams could be formed based categorization factor suitable to the project scenario, for example based on business group, or based on product or business application grouping, or based on technology.

Prioritization

Prioritization is an important activity in Scrumban, it determines the order in which work requests are to be picked up by the team. It is recommended to do the prioritization activity before the planning event.

The work requests that flow into Planned Work cadence should be prioritized by the Product Owner to keep the business, users, or stakeholder interest in focus. The team will use this priority in building the Sprint backlog, typically picked from the top of the prioritized backlog. The rest of the backlog can be re-prioritized based on the changing business scenarios or other changes in the priorities.

In a typical Software Maintenance scenario, work flows from various channels such as Demand Management (Major and Minor Enhancements, known bug fixes), Service Request Management (Standard Service Requests, Data Fixes, Ad-hoc Report creation, etc.), Incident Management, and Defect Management (defects reported on the enhancements and bug fixes).

The work requests that flow in to Planned Work cadence mostly come from Demand Management and part of Service Request Management. This work should be prioritized by a prioritization committee, or can sometimes be rule-based with oversight from the committee. It requires a well-defined rules framework to assign the priority upstream and fine tune as the work requests flow in to the final stages of prioritization.

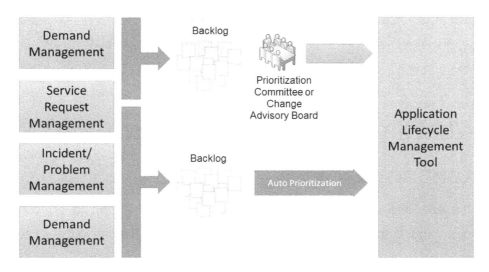

Prioritization

The work requests that flow into Unplanned Work cadence typically carry priority as set by the requester, moderated by Level 1 and Level 2 support teams, and overseen by the Product Owner. In cases where the number of work requests flowing into the cadence is high, an automated process should be devised.

In case of a low number of work requests, a manual process would suffice. Automated prioritization can be achieved through setting certain priority attributes (high medium or low) using prioritization policies. Generally, when Unplanned Work cadence experiences a high flow of requests, there may not be an opportunity to prioritize the work manually. The Product Owner should have the ability to alter any priorities, but only in exceptional situations.

On a normal day, work requests should be picked up from the top of the prioritized backlog, which is pre-ordered based on certain policies defined by the Product Owner. These policies could be based on the Work Request attributes – Category, Priority, Impact, or Need-By-Date. For example, a Service Request with Emergency category with an earlier Need-By-Date will be at the top of the list.

What if you are already on Scrum or Kanban?

This scenario of the team already on Scrum or Kanban is an added advantage. It is easy to implement Scrumban by slowly shifting the existing practices to align with Scrumban principles and practices. Since Scrumban is based on both Scrum and Kanban, the transition will be much smoother.

Teams already following Scrum

The teams already following Scrum can continue to follow Scrum, identify the work that is unplanned or needs unplanned deliveries, or the work that goes through a change in priorities, and channel such tentative work through parallel cadence.

Teams already following Kanban

The teams already following Kanban would have to slowly start adapting to Scrum practices with Kanban assisting in implementing the pull effect.

When can Scrumban work wonders?

The Scrumban methodology is best suited to the Software Maintenance or event–driven work such as help desk/product support. In certain situations, when Scrum is challenged by the workflow issues, Scrumban comes in handy to rescue the situation.

Kanban vs Scrumban

There is no prescribed role in Kanban and no daily meetings required. But in Scrumban, daily meetings can help to ensure continuous workflow. Review and retrospective meetings are not significant in Kanban whereas in Scrumban it works in favor of process improvement. In both Kanban and Scrumban, the workflow is continuous, but Scrumban adds improved predictability through uninterrupted flow of regular planned work.

Quick snapshot of Scrumban features

Scrumban features are listed below to show where they are applicable, but some of these can be consolidated into one feature or applied as separate features. For example, Daily Stand-up meeting can be combined depending on the project scenario.

- **Ceremonies:** Daily Stand-up, Sprint Planning, Sprint Review, and Sprint Retrospective.
- **Product Backlog:** List of prioritized Work Requests, List of Just-in-Time cards.
- **Time-boxed iterations:** Required for the planned work and not required for the unplanned work.
- **Cross-functional teams:** Required for the planned work and optional for unplanned work.

- **Charts:** Burn-down chart for planned work and Cumulative Flow Diagram for unplanned work.

- **Metrics:** Lead Time.

- **Estimations:** Required for planned work, and optional for unplanned work.

- **Sharing sprint backlog/ board across teams:** It is only shared with those within the team, not shared across.

- **Prescribed roles:** Product Owner, Scrumban Master, Team Member, and Specialist.

- **Life of the board:** Resets, after each iteration for planned work; persistent and never ending for unplanned work.

- **Prioritization:** Requires a prioritized product backlog for planned work; automatic prioritization or manual prioritization depending on the scenario.

- **Rework or changes:** Only possible in the next sprint for planned work, added to the board (To Do column) at any time under unplanned work.

How does it address our current problem?

Three focus areas: Visualizing the workflow to remove any possible bottlenecks and impediments, finishing work in progress before adding new work items, and managing the high priority items without disrupting the planned work.

Two main cadences: The first takes care of planned Software Maintenance requests, time-boxed or fixed delivery frequency, and delivered every 1 or

2 or 4 weeks depending on the sprint cycle, and without any interruptions. The second cadence takes care of unplanned work in a Just-in-Time fashion with focus on improving workflow.

Two charts: Burn-down chart shows the remaining work to be completed projecting a possible iteration completion date, and the cumulative flowchart shows the average lead time trend and flow efficiency.

This is just an introduction to the Scrumban model, later chapters would describe the implementation aspects of Scrumban in a project.

***

The

Implementation

Chapter 7

So, how do we slice the elephant?

"Step by step and the thing is done." - Charles
Atlas

So far, we have seen how Software Maintenance is different and how Scrumban can address the challenges posed to make things better. But how would one go about implementing Scrumban in a project? Implementing Scrumban in a Software Maintenance project might look like a Herculean task, but the following chapters would give you a perspective on step by step implementation to make it easy and simple.

It is quite natural to go through a dilemma when you are about to change the status-quo. By this time, you would have tried everything you know and the situation seems beyond your control. Trying something new always raises a certain amount of skepticism. You often hear comments such as "our project is different" or "these methods look good on paper only" or "we tried different flavors of this, they did not work." One important enabler that you need to keep in mind while getting down to implement Scrumban is organizational change management. A good organizational change management is the key to successful implementation. A well prepared Scrumban implementation plan must have a good Organization Change Management (OCM) focus.

You must have:
- Well documented principles, policies, and frameworks

- Focused approach to upgrade people skills and competencies on Scrum, Kanban, and Scrumban

It is not possible to cover OCM in this publication. It is recommended to follow the standard OCM framework defined within your organization to make implementation smoother.

Prerequisites

Assuming that you get past the above checks, are there any prerequisites for Scrumban implementation? Yes, there are few prerequisite conditions that must be fulfilled to ensure a smooth and successful implementation of Scrumban. Some of these might be already in place in case you are already using Scrum or Kanban. Before you start implementing, make sure you have these prerequisites in place.

Know-how of Scrum and Kanban

Scrumban implementation requires a good understanding of Scrum and Kanban methodologies. At least a few key team members must be trained and certified on Scrum and Kanban to make the implementation successful. The team should also have a Scrum Master with good experience in running Scrum teams. The Scrum Master must have a good understanding of Kanban.

Client approval

The team must have an explicit approval from the Product Owner (PO) and stakeholders from the client's organization on the principles, policies and practices of Scrumban. Client's understanding and agreement on various practices would be key to achieving the potential benefits. Without client approval, implementing this model would be futile.

Self-organizing team

Not to mention, the team with the drive to do something different and to achieve better results in their day to day Software Maintenance work is the most important prerequisite. When I say team, it is everyone who is involved starting from Product Owner(s), managers, developers, testers, and other technical team members. Everyone in the team should understand Scrumban and believe that it will help them improve their effectiveness.

One last check before you take the plunge

It is always better to do one last check on whether or not Scrumban is the correct approach for your project. Given below is a short list of questions for your evaluation. If most of the responses to the questions are "Yes," then you can take the plunge. If not, you can still read this book to be prepared when you get in to this situation.

1. Is your Software Maintenance and Support team always working on high priority work items?
2. Are there other regular work items which must be delivered on-time without getting impacted by these unplanned and emergency work items?

3. Does your team miss or postpone release dates more often than usual?

Here are the 5 steps to start Scrumban in your project.

1	**Visualizing work and workflow**
2	**Setting Scrumban flow**
3	**Setting Scrumban system**
4	**Defining Team, Artifacts &, Ceremonies**
5	**Setting Metrics and Charts**

***

Chapter 8

Step 1 - Visualizing work and workflow

"To accomplish great things we must first dream,
then visualize, then plan... believe... act!" - Alfred A.
Montapert

Scrumban advocates continuing with existing processes, making incremental changes, and respecting current roles. It is not mandatory to change workflow, roles, responsibilities, and practices to implement Scrumban. Continue with what you have and make incremental and evolutionary changes to get to the Scrumban way. This chapter covers the first and the most important step in this journey, visualization of the work items and their workflows, which provides the preliminary and vital inputs for Scrumban implementation.

The work

Identifying the work item types in scope under Software Maintenance may seem like a simple step, but it needs utmost attention. Each and every work type, however small or big, must be identified.

Broadly these work items should include:
- Enhancements or Planned work requests such as Software Enhancements or known non-emergency software defects.

- Non-enhancements or Unplanned work requests such as emergency software defect fixes, emergency data fixes, responding to queries, testing requests, and impact analysis requests should be identified.

Given below is the list of typical work item types of Software Maintenance projects, but this is not a complete list.

Major Enhancements are mostly enhancements to add a major feature or module to the software. These could fall into any of the four types of maintenance. These enhancements are typically measured in terms of "Themes" with underlying epics and user stories.

Medium Enhancements are additional features to the software, sub features under a main module or feature, which are measured in terms of "Epics" with underlying user stories.

Minor Enhancements are minor changes to an existing feature or a new sub-feature or entirely new features but small in size. These enhancements are measured in terms of user stories.

Service requests are generally listed services in the catalogue; for example, generating an ad-hoc report or setting up a new department or setting up a campaign or providing user access to an application or recruiting a new employee. These typically require the IT team to execute a special function or run scripts or batch jobs or execute certain steps to fulfill the service request raised by the users.

Bug Fixes involve analyzing, coding, testing, and deploying the production defects reported by the users or stakeholders. These may include a simple one line change to the code or rewriting an entire function. Depending on the impact of these fixes, the team might need to do only system testing or do a regression testing to validate no impact to any other existing functionality.

Data Fixes are changes to the existing data; these are done as a work around to a problem or correcting data corruption of an upstream system on a continuous basis. These could be one time fixes or recurring ones to be run with certain frequency till the original problem, which is causing this data corruption, is fixed.

Impact analysis requests originate from other groups to conduct an impact analysis on the software due to changes that need to be performed as part of other change requests. Sometimes these are also requested to assess and estimate the impact of any change to help with the prioritization and planning processes.

Problem analysis and resolution requests are raised in a production support scenario where there is a problem and L1 and L2 teams are not able to find a resolution and the maintenance team is requested to investigate by going through the code to identify a workaround or a resolution.

User queries are raised through a variety of avenues. Some come through help desk or service desk and others come through various communication channels viz. questions from portals or websites, emails, or chat help tools. These sometimes may take significant effort to respond to.

Production validation requests or Testing requests or Production text changes (PTC) are work requests that need no programming effort from the team. These are mostly text changes or XML changes, which do not change the behavior of the software.

The tasks

The tasks are of two types in Software Maintenance: the first type of tasks is related to Work Requests; the second type of tasks is not related to Work Requests, but the team needs to perform these tasks as part of the project. For convenience, the first type can be called Story Tasks and the second type can be called Story-less Tasks. These can be tracked on the main board or a separate task board. The task board is discussed in detail in the later sections.

Story Tasks

The typical tasks under the enhancement type of work requests are Analysis, Design, Coding, and Testing. During the planning meeting, each enhancement should be broken down into these detailed tasks to be performed. In cases where there are multiple components to be developed, these tasks would depend on the number of components and type of the component. For example, an enhancement involves one web page, one server component, and one data component. Each of these components needs to have associated analysis, design, coding, and testing tasks to complete the work request. There could be additional tasks such as code review, integration testing, and performance testing.

For Bug Fixes, the tasks could be Impact Analysis, Coding, and Testing. The tasks for Data Fixes could be Impact Analysis, Scripting, and Data Validation. Each work type should be analyzed and basic tasks need to be kept as a template to be considered during the planning meeting.

Story-less Tasks

The Story-less tasks are the tasks which cannot be related to any story or work request, they are configuration management related, packaging related, environment set up related, tool configurations, reviews and so on. It is essential to identify these during the planning meeting and add them to the task board. Very often these are missed out during the planning which leads to delays.

The workflow

After the work items are identified, visualize the workflow of these work items in terms of the specific stages through which work item traverses to reach to the final stage of its lifecycle. The main objective is to derive generic flows from the identified specific flows. The following figure illustrates an example of a typical Software Maintenance work request workflow:

Example of Software Maintenance work request workflow

The Product Owner adds work requests to the backlog, and then the Product Owner or prioritization committee prioritizes them for the next release. The team picks up the work requests and they are moved from one stage to another viz. analysis, design, build, testing, and User Acceptance Testing, and finally they get deployed.

There could be different ways the work flows through various stages depending on the work request and the project scenario. In scrum projects, typically, the team is cross-functional. All the stages are therefore covered by one team member.

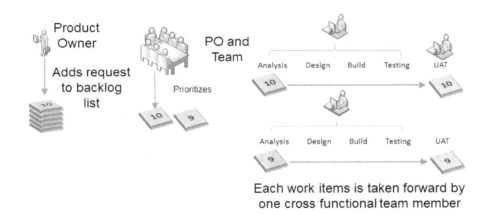

Each work items is taken forward by one cross functional team member

Typical Scrum workflow

Similarly, a software maintenance project may have another type of workflow for different work items, which needs more specialized skills at each stage. Figure below shows various stages of a Kanban workflow.

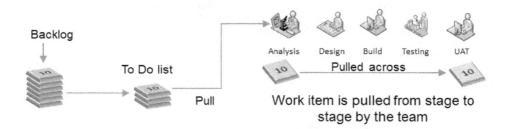

Typical Kanban workflow

In some scenarios, the work item may not go through elaborate stages as shown above. It would typically have only one stage of "Doing" and moved to completion. Standard service requests fall into this kind of scenario. The key aspect here is to identify various workflows and abstract these stages so that you have generic workflow stages across the project.

Visualization should result in defining workflow stages

The visualization step is to study various workflows in your project and abstract them into one or two generic workflows. It is also necessary to visualize the start and end of the workflow, including all the interface points with other teams in the workflow.

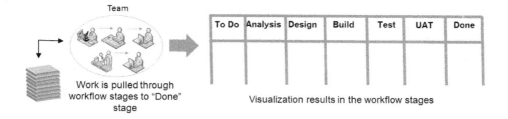

Visualization of workflow stages

Sometimes it is very difficult to come up with a generic workflow for Planned Work and Un-planned cadences, or across various types of work requests that are processed in the project. In such cases, simple workflow stages can be defined to start with, which can be modified in the later stages.

It is also possible to create sub-stages in a certain flow, but restrict it to a major cadence such as Planned and Unplanned, or Enhancements and Non-Enhancements. This would make the model easier to implement with WIP limits at work stage level.

	Backlog	To Do	Design		Coding		Test		Done
			Doing	Done	Doing	Done	Doing	Done	
Enhancements Or Planned Work									
	Backlog	To Do	Design		Coding		Test		Done
			Doing	Done	Doing	Done	Doing	Done	
Non-Enhancements Or Unplanned Work									

Doing and Done columns at every stage

On each main cadence, make sure you have "Doing" and "Done" columns whereever necessary to facilitate the pull. For example, Design stage should have a "Doing" and "Done" column so that the Coding team member pulls the items from Analysis stage "Done" column into Coding stage "Doing" column and starts working.

Applying Kanban principles on a cadence

The real strength of Scrumban comes from applying Kanban principles over Scrum model. Adding "Doing" and "Done" for the execution stages and implementing WIP Limit creates pull effect within the Scrum model.

It is also recommended to have an Expedite cadence to enable the team to deliver some of the emergency work requests in a fast lane for anytime deployment.

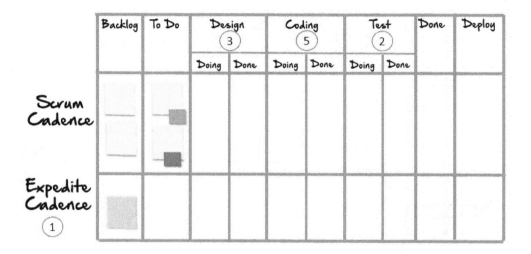

Adding Expedite cadence

Planned Work cadence will deliver with the Sprint frequency, whereas the Expedite cadence will deliver at any time frequency as needed by the business. By the end of this step, the work item types, related tasks and their workflowstages should have been identified.

Keep DevOps in mind

Whether you already implemented DevOps or not, it is very important to understand and visualize the deployment stages to make this model comprehensive. Remember, the goal is not to make the Software Maintenance alone efficient, the goal is to make the entire lifecycle efficient, starting from demand to deploy.

These are some of the basic implementation aspects of Scrumban for Software Maintenance. Ensure you take this as guidelines in visualizing work and workflow and create your model. There could be scenarios which force you to take a slightly different direction, but make sure you adhere to the basic principles of Scrumban so that you don't lose the effectiveness of this model.

Summary

1. Identify the work item types in scope under Software Maintenance.

2. Visualize the workflow of each work type to identify the stages traversed to reach to the final stage of the lifecycle.

3. Abstract the work flow stages to finalize the stages relevant to the project scenario. The stages could be different for Planned Work and Unplanned cadences.

4. Apply Kanban stages 'To Do' and 'Doing' to Scrum stages to create pull mechanism.

5. Add an Expedite cadence to handle the work requests which need immediate attention.

***

Chapter 9

Step 2 – Setting up Scrumban flow

"Working hard and working smart sometimes can
be two different things." - Byron Dorgan

Until now, we have seen how to set the workflow stages or columns on the Scrumban board. Now let us identify the rows on the board. These are also called cadences or swim lanes under two cadences already defined. Enhancements cadence and Non-Enhancements cadence. It is not always required to set up sub cadences; in a simple scenario you can work with just two cadences. It means that the work items that flow into your system are all of homogeneous nature, same size, same priority, and same source. In reality, this scenario is very rare; therefore, it is almost certain that Software Maintenance will have multiple sub-cadences. This is the step that needs utmost caution to start in the right direction in your Scrumban journey, there is always room for improvement to fine tune your model, but it is essential to do a thorough analysis before you setup your first version of the Scrumban system.

Setting up Cadences

Setting up cadences in Scrumban can be very tricky. It entirely depends on the way your project is organized, or the type of work, or the type of Service Level Agreements or other similar factors. It is essential to analyze all these factors to set the right Scrumban flow. At a high level, the Work Requests should flow through different prioritization processes into these two defined cadences.

Typically, enhancement work is planned and sizable. These work requests should go through a prioritization process. Once prioritized, these work requests go into the prioritized backlog. The requests are further prioritized to form sprint backlog and moved into To-Do column for the team to start the Sprint. Once the sprint is completed, the sprint planning meeting would take the next set of work requests from the prioritized backlog for the next sprint backlog. This repeats in a continuous cycle. The sub-cadences under Planned work cadence would be one for each individual work request. This would enable the tasks related to these individual work requests to flow into their respective sub-cadences. It is not mandatory to have these sub-cadences. That is only required if the board is used as a task board.

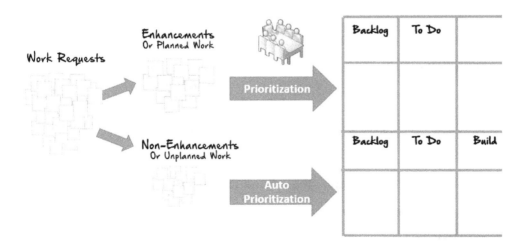

Setting Cadences for Scrumban

When it comes to Unplanned work, which directly flows into the backlog column, having a manual prioritization for these work requests is very tedious as these are small in size and more in numbers. It is better to have an automatic prioritization based on certain predefined rules. The way sub-cadences are defined could be based on the class of service, or business area, or technology. It is recommended to prioritize these work requests automatically, based on the business criticality and priority attributes set by the requester, and a moderator arbitrating these at the source system.

A Scrumban Master can play a role to ensure the automatic prioritization is effective, and override in any exception cases by increasing or decreasing the priorities appropriately.

Analysing Demand and Allocating Capacity

For each type of work identified, the amount of work that flows into the project needs to be analyzed. It is best if you have historical data to make a quantitative analysis. If you do not have any past data, then a derived subjective analysis will suffice to get going.

The demand analysis provides inputs to form the cadences and the kind of team structure required to handle the demand. For example, in the technology based model, the demand analysis would provide the approximate capacity required to handle requests specific to a particular technology. This would help the manager to allocate team members according to their technical skills. Similarly, in other models, the capacity can be allocated based on the business domain skills, or expertise in handling work item types such as data fixes, user queries, and service requests or capacity can be allocated based on the skills in handling expedite or urgent class requests.

Irrespective of which dimension or combination of dimensions (work item based, service class based, business based, or technology based) the demand is organized, the work in Software Maintenance projects can be categorized as planned and unplanned at a high level.

Planned work: involves major and minor enhancement requests, known defects, and other technical requests under adaptive and perfective category. They require a good amount of planning, analysis, and design. They typically follow your development life cycle phases. Though they are not urgent requests, such requests need to be delivered before a deadline. Their inflow can be predicted, or capped according to the capacity available.

Unplanned work: mainly high priority bug fixes and data fixes, production text changes, user queries, impact analysis requests, estimation requests, and testing requests. Most do not need extensive programming effort, but require immediate attention. Unplanned work comes without any notice. It is very hard to predict and plan around such requests.

		Design		Coding		Test		Done
Backlog	To Do	Doing	Done	Doing	Done	Doing	Done	Done

Enhancements
Or Planned Work

40% of
capacity

		Design		Coding		Test		Done
Backlog	To Do	Doing	Done	Doing	Done	Doing	Done	Done

Non-Enhancements
Or Unplanned Work

60% of
capacity

Allocating capacity

Drawing just two cadences as shown below would also be a good starting point in Scrumban implementation. Based on the demand analysis, the effort spent on these two categories could potentially decide the allocation of capacity. For example, approximate effort spent on planned requests is 60%. The remaining 40% is spent on unplanned requests. The team can be structured based on this ratio. The team working on the planned effort will plan and execute the way any Scrum team operates with time-boxed iterations. The other team works on the unplanned requests in the Kanban way, pulling the work based on WIP limits.

Either way, various patterns of work items that are flowing into the project must be understood and grouped by various dimensions. Depending on what suits your project scenario, the sub-cadences should be formed as described later in this section. This is only to provide a few samples for your consideration, not to prescribe these as models. The key point is to understand the demand and split it into different cadences based on the dimension that suits your project the most.

The capacity is the available maintenance team's bandwidth with regard to the scope of the project. This available capacity needs to be reserved for various cadences based on the analysis of the historical data of requests received, or by an anecdotally derived subjective analysis. This allocation of capacity can be fine-tuned as we go along the Scrumban journey.

Depending on the work that flows into the scope of the Software Maintenance, the capacity needs to be allocated. Following are the four sample dimensions to consider while conducting the demand analysis. In case there is no demand data to conduct this level of analysis, move ahead with certain assumptions and fine tune the capacity to reach an optimum allocation.

Work Type based model

Visualization of work should have identified the work item types relevant to your project viz. change requests, bug fixes, service requests, alarms. Analyze the work requests using work item type dimension. You should be able to identify the cadences or swim lanes or rows that you need on your Scrumban flow. For example, change requests could further be classified into minor and major change requests; bug fixes could be small, medium or large.

MONTH	Bug Fixes	Change Requests	Service Requests
Jan	20	10	42
Feb	22	11	41
Mar	24	14	39
Apr	21	12	38
May	28	9	44
Jun	23	12	36

	Analysis	Design	Build	Test	UAT	Done
Bug Fixes						
Change Requests						
Service Requests						

Work type based model

Analyze the past data in terms of work request types and group them into fewer Work Type cadences. This mode may not be suitable in case you end up with too many or too few categories.

Class of Service based model

The work items could be categorized based on the service class viz. priority based, criticality based, or impact based. The work that flows is mostly based on the service class and you see strong reason(s) to base your demand analysis on this dimension. You should consider this dimension to conduct your analysis.

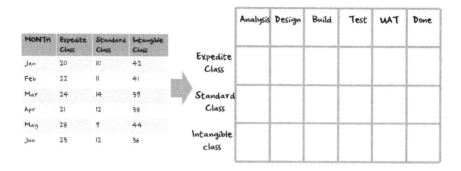

MONTH	Expedite Class	Standard Class	Intangible Class
Jan	20	10	42
Feb	22	11	41
Mar	24	14	39
Apr	21	12	38
May	28	9	44
Jun	23	12	36

	Analysis	Design	Build	Test	UAT	Done
Expedite Class						
Standard Class						
Intangible class						

Class of Service based model

In case the past data analysis shows that the Class of Service is of primary focus in your scenario, group them into fewer Classes of Service cadences such as Expedite, Standard, Fixed Date, and Intangible.

Business based model

The work items should be categorized based on the business portfolio or business process or application group or any other business categorization. The work that flows is mostly based on the business and you can see strong reasons to base your demand analysis on this dimension. You should consider this dimension for your analysis.

MONTH	Back Office	Front Office	Sales & Marketing
Jan	20	10	42
Feb	22	11	41
Mar	24	14	39
Apr	21	12	38
May	28	9	44
Jun	23	12	36

	Analysis	Design	Build	Test	UAT	Done
Back Office						
Front Office						
Sales & Marketing						

Business based model

In case the past data analysis shows that business areas are of primary focus in your scenario, you can group them into fewer Business Areas as cadences; for example, Back Office, Front Office, Sales and Marketing.

Technology based model

The work items could be categorized based on the technology viz. legacy or web based or mobility or client server or middleware or enterprise applications. The work that flows is mostly based on the technology and you can see strong reasons to base your demand analysis on this dimension. You should consider this dimension for your analysis.

MONTH	Legacy	Web	Middleware
Jan	20	10	42
Feb	22	11	41
Mar	24	14	39
Apr	21	12	38
May	28	9	44
Jun	23	12	36

	Analysis	Design	Build	Test	UAT	Done
Legacy						
Web						
Middleware						

Technology based model

In case the past data analysis shows that technology areas are of primary focus in your scenario, group them into fewer Technology Areas as cadences; for example, Legacy, Web, and Middleware.

IMPORTANT: It has proved very effective to have an Expedite class cadence or a Fast Lane irrespective of the model you follow in forming the cadences.

Building Planned Work cadence

The planned work cadence of the Scrumban is mostly enhancements and known defects, and is the least interruption prone. The work is picked up from the prioritized backlog and slotted into multiple releases. Each release is split into time-boxed multiple sprints.

Depending on the demand on the Planned Work that flows in to the team, you need to decide whether the Scrumban team would be able to handle the volume. Typically, an unplanned cadence team cannot have more than 10 team members. In case you need multiple teams to handle the demand, you need to adopt Scrum of Scrums or Scaled Agile to handle the demand. The key difference is to have a multi-team stand-up. Hold a short meeting to keep various teams abreast of cross team integration aspects across the software portfolio. Generally, a select member from each Scrum team would represent at the scrum of scrums.

These Scrums can be decided based on your demand analysis and capacity allocation. You should form various Scrums to channel the demand into various cadences and rolling up to Scrum of Scrum to move the entire demand forward.

Build unplanned work cadence

The unplanned work cadence of Scrumban handles work that flows with certain priorities based on the policies defined. Depending on the model which is most suited, the unplanned cadence will have the requests automatically prioritized according to the model most suited for your scenario. To form the unplanned work cadence, identify one model or a combination of the models discussed earlier such as work type based model, business based model, service class based model, or technology based model. Service class based is most suited unless there is strong reason to choose another model or a combination model to form the cadence and underlying sub-cadences.

Service Class based model

Service Class based model categorizes the work requests based on Class of Service defined in Software Maintenance. Every Class of Service should have its own policies to prioritize based on the business impact and the cost of delay. This enables the team to streamline the flow of work to deliver according to the business needs. Implementing Service Class based model positively impacts flow efficiency, lead times, customer satisfaction, and team motivation.

A Class of Service policy should include the following aspects:

- Visibility– Description of methods to improve the visibility of the Class of Service, such as Color coding of cards, a dedicated cadence (row on the board)
- Prioritization – Description of the method followed to define the prioritization methods, such as FIFO method, Expected Delivery Date, Business Priority

- Estimation requirements – Policy of the estimation methodology to be followed in line with the overall direction of the implementation model, such as no estimation, or prescribed estimation model

- Impact – Description of the impact of not delivering the work requests, in terms of risk to the business and cost of delay on a time scale

Expedite class

The Expedite class requests are special work requests or tasks of high business impact. These are work requests that are typically emergencies, business is down, and need to be fixed with all the resources available.

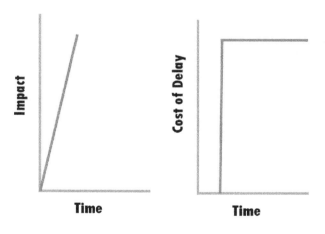

Impact of Expedite class [1]

The impact of doing or not doing an Expedite class request is immediate and cost of delay is very high. The Expedite Class of Service can be very

---

[1] David Anderson's Kanban book discusses in detail the impact and cost of delay of a particular class

disruptive to flow due to its urgent nature. Use a dedicated lane to protect some capacity against these disruptions and then limit the number of expedites on the board at any given time. This allows servicing the Expedite class while minimizing the impact on the other Service Classes.

There is a risk of swarming this lane with delayed items and genuine expedites. Setting a WIP limit is mandatory to restrict the impact of this class on other work in the flow. It is noticed that large amount of Expedite class requests flow into the system on some occasions, as a sign of low trust in the team's ability to deliver reliably. So the business / user group's response is to make everything Expedite class. The only way to resolve this challenge is to meet the commitments for other Class of Services, which would establish the trust needed to overcome this emotional response.

Expedite Policies

- Limit the expedite requests to one or two at any given time
- The best resource on the team must pull Expedite requests immediately. The work on hand will be put on hold or on blocked items list to process the expedite request
- At any point in the workflow, the WIP limit may be exceeded in order to accommodate the expedited request. Capacity is not being held in reserve for expediting
- Emergency deployment to be planned to move the expedite request into production as soon as possible
- White cards can be used for Expedite class requests

Fixed Delivery Date class

The Fixed Delivery Date class is work request that needs to be delivered by a certain date. Missing the date would have a high business impact. For example, when upgrading an Operating System with a newer version, the web services do not work unless the upgrade is made on a specific date. This would significantly impact the business in terms of loss of web-based sales.

The impact is very high after the deadline, so this class of requests needs to be prioritized early to meet the deadline and avoid the high cost of delay.

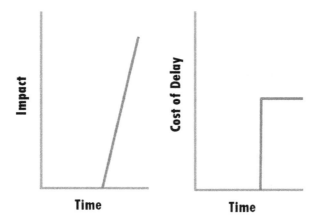

Impact of Fixed Delivery Date class [2]

Policies

- The required delivery date is displayed on the bottom right-hand corner of the card

---

[2] David Anderson's Kanban book discusses in detail the impact and cost of delay of a particular class

- Fixed delivery date items are subject to some analysis and an estimate of size and effort may be made to assess the flow time. If the item is large, it may be broken up into smaller items. Each smaller item will be assessed independently to see whether it qualifies as a fixed delivery date item

- Fixed delivery date items are held in the backlog until they are selected for the input queue, close to the ideal point for them to be delivered on time given the flow-time estimate

- Fixed delivery date items are pulled in preference over other, less risky items. They are pulled before standard or intangible class items

- Fixed delivery date items must adhere to the WIP limit. Fixed delivery date items queue for release when they are complete and ready for release. They are released in a regularly scheduled release just prior to their required delivery date

- If a fixed delivery date item gets behind, and release on the desired date is at risk, its class of service may be promoted to an expedite request

- Fixed delivery date items use purple cards

Standard Class

Most items needed should be treated as standard class items. Cost of delay is low, but accelerates before leveling out. Provide a reasonable lead time expectation.

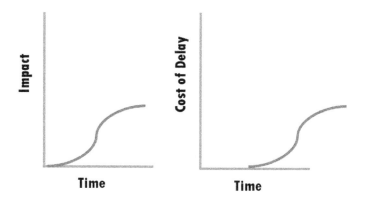

Impact of Standard class [3]

Policies

- Standard class items are prioritized into the input queue based on an agreed-upon mechanism, such as democratic voting, and are typically selected based on their cost of delay or business value

- Standard class items use first in, first out (FIFO) queuing as they are pulled through the system. Typically, when given an option, a team member pulls the oldest standard class item if there is no expedite or fixed date item to choose in preference

- Standard class items queue for release when they are complete and ready for release. They are released in the next scheduled release

- No estimation is performed to determine a level of effort or flow time

- Standard class items may be analyzed for order of magnitude in size. Typically classified as small (a few days), medium (a week or two), and large (perhaps months). Classes of service should be

---

[3] David Anderson's Kanban book discusses in detail the impact and cost of delay of a particular class

113

clearly, visually displayed by using, for example, different colored cards to represent the class of service or different swim lanes on the card wall

- Large items may be broken down into smaller items. Each item may be queued and flowed separately
- Standard class items use yellow cards

Intangible class

These are important and needed, but there is no tangible short-term cost of delay. Sometimes, the cost of delay may be significant, but is not incurred until much later; these are important but not urgent requests.

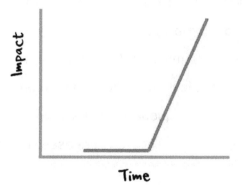

Impact of Intangible class [4]

Policies

---

[4] David Anderson's Kanban book discusses in detail the impact and cost of delay of a particular class

- Intangible class items are prioritized into the input queue based on an agreed-upon mechanism, such as democratic voting, and are typically selected based on some longer-term impact or cost of delay

- Intangible class items are pulled through the system in an ad hoc fashion. Team members may choose to pull an intangible class item regardless of its entry date, so long as a higher-class item is not available

- Intangible class items queue for release when they are complete and ready for release. They are released in the next scheduled release or are held to be assembled with other items

- No estimation is performed to determine a level of effort or flow time

- Intangible class items may be analyzed for large items and may be broken down into smaller items. Each item may be queued and flowed separately

- Typically, an intangible class item is put aside in order to process an expedite request

- It may not be necessary to offer a service-level agreement with intangible class items. If it is necessary, it should be a significantly more pliable agreement than that offered for standard class items. For example, 60 days with 50 percent due-date performance

- Intangible class items use green cards

Once the Planned and Unplanned cadences are decided the Visual Board should have these two main cadences and sub-cadences depending on your project specific requirements. A typical board is shown below as an example, your board may look different in terms of stages and sub-cadences.

	Backlog	To Do	Analysis		Build		Test		Ready	Deploy
			Doing	Done	Doing	Done	Doing	Done		
Scrumban										
	Backlog	To Do	Analysis		Build		Test		Ready	Deploy
			Doing	Done	Doing	Done	Doing	Done		
EXPEDITE										
STANDARD										
INTANGIBLE										

Typical Scrumban visual board

Setting up Delivery Frequency

Delivery Frequency is the frequency by which work requests are delivered for production deployments. Setting up the Delivery Frequency is the process of analyzing various factors and agreeing upon a delivery frequency between the team and stakeholders. The team will deliver working Software Maintenance releases with this frequency and the stakeholders expect to review and accept them into the production environment.

Most of the times, the day of the delivery is also an agreed upon day of a week or month, e.g., every second Wednesday. This frequency depends on various factors such as availability of outage windows with less interruption to the business, overhead effort required in deploying into the production environment, and availability of testers to do the User Acceptance Test.

Start with something

Based on data and inputs from the stakeholders, decide on a delivery frequency that works well for stakeholders and the team. It is very important to establish it very early in the life cycle of a project. Many scrum projects generally follow 30 days sprints, but more recently teams have been successful with two-week or even one-week sprints. Short delivery frequency will be more suitable for Software Maintenance projects. However, while trying to determine the appropriate stimulus-to-response time for your project, consider the following criteria:

- Stakeholders: how often can they provide feedback and guidance?

- Environmental factors: criticality of the software, demand for changes from the users, support team availability, cost of deployment

- The team: Scrum experience, Technical capabilities (such as automated acceptance testing, TDD, automated releases, etc.), and ability to decompose work

Experiment with it

Experiment with the delivery frequency, determine an optimal stimulus-to-response cycle, and refine it to suit the project scenario. The initial iterations should be set based on the business need, costs involved in the release and deployment, availability of testing and other resources, and various other factors specific to the project. Once the delivery frequency is set up, it should be discussed at every retrospective meeting to identify any need to change it. Get inputs from stakeholders and others involved to make these changes. It typically takes two to three iterations to finalize the frequency.

Keep it consistent

Though setting up delivery frequency is an evolving process, once finalized it should be fixed and strictly adhered to. Keep it consistent. Consistency is very important because it helps you find a rhythm, makes your process repeatable and measurable, and allows you to understand the flow and make changes to other parameters to improve the flow efficiency.

By the end of this step, decide on the delivery frequency for the planned cadence and the unplanned cadence. Typically, planned cadence delivery frequency will be longer than the delivery cadence of the unplanned cadence. Planned work iteration may vary from 2 weeks to 4 weeks, and unplanned work delivery frequency may vary from 1 week to 2 weeks.

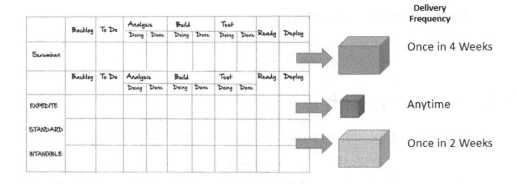

Delivery Frequency

Setting a delivery frequency also helps in aligning the other processes of UAT, Performance Testing, Systems Testing, and Deployment.

Setting the Replenishment Frequency

Replenishment Frequency is the agreed-upon frequency established between the team and stakeholders to determine what should go into the prioritized backlog.

1. Setting up input cadence is an evolving process in the beginning, but later should be fixed and strictly followed

2. Initially, it should be set up according to the business need to deploy changes, availability of the stakeholders, and various other factors specific to the project

3. Once the input cadence is set up, it should be discussed in retrospective meetings to identify any need to change it, with input from stakeholders and other involved members

In Scrumban, setting up replenishment frequency varies between the two main cadences – Planned Work and Unplanned Work. The replenishment frequency for Planned Work depends on the sprint cycle and is no different from how Scrum teams practice. The release planning meeting should prioritize work for 5–6 sprints, typically done by the Product Owner (PO) and the stakeholders.

The replenishment frequency for Unplanned Work should be automatic, but may be aligned with Scrum replenishment frequency to prioritize the known defects, standard requests, and some intangible requests to replenish the backlog. There are multiple ways this can be achieved.

1. Having standard policies to set the severity and priority to the work items, which would direct the team to pick up work items from the top of the to-do list.

2. Just in time (JIT) replenishment meetings to prioritize the backlog. This would work well if the availability of the Product Owner and stakeholders is not a constraint.

3. Expedite cadence replenishment is based on the highest business priority. Any work request is marked as high business priority and high severity will be categorized as Expedite class in the backlog.

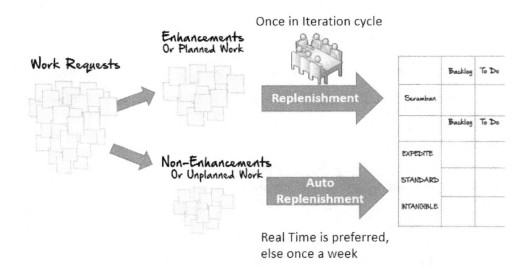

Replenishment types

There could be many other ways to decide on the replenishment frequency. Adopt whatever suits your project scenario the most and fine-tune it.

Setting the WIP Limits

Setting up of WIP limits or Work-In-Progress limits is the most important step of Scrumban. This is the key to reaping the benefits of the model. Some projects have implemented Scrumban without strictly adhering to WIP limits, and the results have not been promising.

WIP limit denotes the maximum number of work items in a given column of workflow stages across the cadences. These stages are represented by columns in the current context. There are many reasons to believe that WIP limits help in improving the flow.

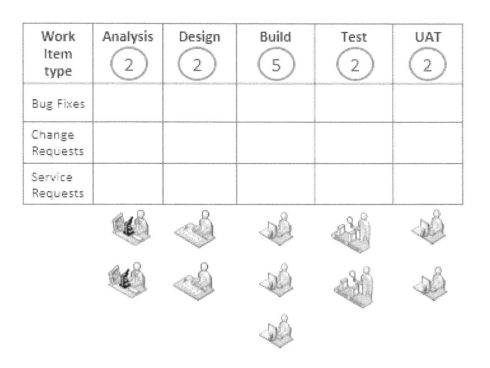

Work Item type	Analysis	Design	Build	Test	UAT
	2	2	5	2	2
Bug Fixes					
Change Requests					
Service Requests					

Illustration of WIP limits

WIP limits ensure that the team keeps a steady rhythm without overloading. It is proven that by focusing on only one task, you would achieve better completion time than by working on two tasks at the same time. In addition, when you have a higher number of in-progress work requests a team member has to switch between several tasks, which is counter-productive.

Steps to setup the WIP limit

- Do the analysis of past data.
- Calculate the average workflow rate in each cadence and workflow state.
- Set the limits and fine tune to increase the flow rate.
- Make it a continuous improvement activity to study the flow efficiency and identify if any change to the WIP limit is necessary.
- WIP limit can be decided based on the number of people working at each workflow stage.
- It also depends on how many concurrent work items each person can handle. It is advised to keep it to the minimum; one item per person is ideal but 3 is a practical number.
- WIP limit should be monitored and corrected to improve the flow.

Where do we start?

Typically, WIP limit is derived from the number of persons working on a particular stage. For example, if there are three programmers working on the coding stage, three can be the WIP limit to start with. But this is too ideal a scenario, and risks programmers waiting in case of any road blocks for the in-progress work request. Therefore, it is recommended to have a WIP limit of more than one for each team member. The WIP limit for a team member has to be a global WIP limit. If this team member is working across multiple projects, it is recommended to keep the total WIP limit for that person across projects as this limit.

The WIP limit on a stage must not be very high or very low. Very high means the team is working on too many at any point, which defeats the purpose of the model. Too low means the team does not have any scope to switch to the other work requests in case the first one has hit a road block and would take a few minutes or hours to get cleared.

Is it a hard limit or a soft limit?

It depends on how you want to use this control without impacting the utility of the feature. WIP limit can be used to serve as an indicator to streamline the flow, or can be used as a hard limit to focus and pull through the work request. The three ways it can be configured are:

- Can exceed limits – the limits serve only as indicators
- Can exceed limits only with a valid reason – serves as an exception route, but is a hard implementation of the limit
- Cannot exceed the limit – serves as a control to improve the focus and flow efficiency

By the end of this step, WIP limit should be decided for each stage on planned and unplanned cadences.

	Backlog	To Do	Analysis (3)		Build (5)		Test (2)		Ready	Deploy
			Doing	Done	Doing	Done	Doing	Done		
Scrumban										
	Backlog	To Do (5)	Analysis (3)		Build (5)		Test (2)		Ready	Deploy
			Doing	Done	Doing	Done	Doing	Done		
EXPEDITE										
STANDARD										
INTANGIBLE										

WIP limits on Scrumban visual board

Mark the Scrumban board with the WIP limits, refining these limits is an iterative process, once you have the limits enforce them with no exceptions.

Setting the Estimation guidelines and practices

In Scrumban, estimation is the process of determining the time required to complete each work item on the board. For time boxed part of the work items, the estimation is typically done before start of the iteration. Any procedure that is in practice can be continued to start with and can be refined incrementally to better estimation methods. T-shirt sizing estimation or poker method or use case method are some of the methods that are described below for reference.

Generally, the items have to be shorter than the time allocated for the time-boxed iteration. If not, the items are usually split into smaller entities. In

Kanban and Scrumban, estimation is optional. After an item is complete, the team members simply pull the next item from the backlog and proceed with implementing it. Some teams still choose to carry out the estimation in order to have more predictability. An alternative approach to achieve predictability is to make sure that each of the items is about the same size, and therefore can be completed in the same amount of time.

There are many estimation models available in the public domain, some are described below for your reference, but create your own estimation model and perfect it to get the maximum benefit based on the model you adopt. If your team is already following an estimation model, review the model to make sure it does not slowdown the team without adding too much value to the entire process.

T-shirt sizing estimation is the best where work item size varies

Many teams are dealing with work of various sizes. If you do a frequency analysis of your data, you will probably see clusters of data. In the picture below, we have three clusters. Rather than spending significant time on complex assessments to support estimations, the team can rapidly assign tasks into these clusters. We call this T-Shirt size estimating. Cluster similar work into XS, S, M, L, and XL. You may decide that you do not accept XL tasks without decomposition or require breaking the tasks down. Then determine estimates for each size based on Mean + 1 Standard Deviation for each of the clusters. You can determine some simple process for assigning work into one of the T-Shirt sizes.

This will not give you perfect estimates. Perfect estimates are almost impossible to determine. Additionally, Cycle Time Variability is probably impacted more by variation in the system like waiting and rework than anything else. It is impossible to determine the impact of the system by more deeply analyzing the task. With T-Shirt sizing and Cycle Time, you can get as accurate results in minutes instead of months. While not perfectly accurate, it is as meaningful as anything you can do.

Fibonacci points

Most of the Agile Teams estimate their work in Tee Shirt Sizes and do a relative sizing in Fibonacci Numbers at the User Story level. By definition, the first two numbers in the Fibonacci sequence are 0 and 1 (alternatively, 1 and 1), and each subsequent number is the sum of the previous two. Thus a Fibonacci sequence looks like:

0,1,1,2,3,5,8,13,21,34,55,89,144...

Generally, Agile teams do not estimate in terms of hours. Though estimates in hours is good for developers and testers as they do not have to worry about the time factor when working on any piece of work.
They can instead focus on the work itself. The benefit of using the Fibonacci sequence is the ability to reflect the inherent uncertainty in estimating larger

items. It means that the larger the size of the card, the more uncertainty exists around what needs to be done to call the card "done-done."

A Fibonacci sequence grows at about the same rate at which we perceive meaningful changes in magnitude, which could be another reason. In principle, the larger stories can be sliced into smaller ones if possible. But it is not always possible to slice the work to provide business values. Therefore, in keeping a user story larger, we introduce chances for uncertainty. It is not possible to accurately estimate work that takes days versus hours without introducing uncertainty. By doing a Fibonacci sequencing of numbers, we account for such uncertainties.

Estimation is a waste of time?

"Estimation is a waste of time" is true when work item size does not vary a lot. From Kanban's point of view, estimation is one form of wastage of the team's capacity. Estimating all the items that are in the backlog solely for the purpose of business to prioritize the work item is a mere waste. If business wants it, it would be prioritized anyway. And most of the estimates are wrong, because they are based on requirements known at that moment, but the requirements keep evolving over a period.

Consequently, spending too much effort in estimating accurately is a mere waste of time. Instead, the requests can be put into an approximate size, for example T-shirt sizes technique, so that work items are quickly put into one of several predefined sizes (S, M, L, XL, and XS) to help the manager in planning. Or do a little bit of analysis of the work already executed in your project to arrive at a standard number to go with, instead of estimating each of the work items.

With this we completed step two of setting up Scrumban flow. Make sure you have customized all the aspects to your project without losing the effectiveness of this new model.

Summary

1. Analyze demand and allocate capacity accordingly

2. Set up Planned work and Unplanned work cadences based on the model that suits the project requirement. For example, Work Type, Class of Service, Business Type, or Technology.

3. Experiment with delivery frequency and keep it consistent once finalized. Make sure there is a different delivery frequency for planned and unplanned cadences, later ones having higher frequency.

4. Set up Replenishment frequency, refine it in 2-3 iterations and keep it consistent.

5. Experiment with Work In Progress (WIP) limit. Once set up, strictly adhere to the set limit.

6. Establish stimation guidelines and practices, keep them aligned with Lean and Agile practices.

***

Chapter 10

Step 3 - Setting Scrumban system

"If you can't describe what you are doing as a process, you don't know what you're doing." - W. Edwards Deming

Extending on the above quote, if you cannot see what you are doing, you do not know where you are going. Scrumban is all about visualizing work and workflow, monitoring the work moving along various stages, tracking the progress of each team member on the work requests or tasks, and identifying the road blocks or impediments to deliver the work in the most agile and lean fashion.

Scrumban requires the most practical and flexible system. It could be a physical system or a virtual system. Whatever it may be, it needs to be defined and owned by the team, and continuously refined to be made perfect for their projects 'scenario. Some of the important components of Scrumban are discussed below, but these are only to provide a guideline to derive your own components that suit your scenario. There are many tools in the market that would offer various features to implement the following components, but it is recommended to have a physical board as well to get better results to create a visual impact if the team is co-located.

Scrumban Board

The Scrumban board is the center of the universe when it comes to this model. This is where everything is planned, monitored, and tracked. The board should have columns and rows, which are various stages and cadences of the work and work flows through the team. As discussed earlier in Step 1, the main inputs come from visualization of the work and workflow. Visualization of work and workflow would identify various cadences and the corresponding stages. These inputs would help in drawing the workflow stages (vertical columns). After visualizing the workflow for all types of work, decide on the workflow stages at a fairly abstract level.

	Backlog	To Do	Analysis (3)		Build (5)		Test (2)		Ready	Deploy
			Doing	Done	Doing	Done	Doing	Done		
Scrumban										
	Backlog	To Do (5)	Analysis (3)		Build (5)		Test (2)		Ready	Deploy
			Doing	Done	Doing	Done	Doing	Done		
EXPEDITE										
STANDARD										
INTANGIBLE										

Typical Scrumban visual board

For example, all maintenance requests go through analysis, design, build, test, and deployment at an abstract level. Major enhancements might go through an extensive analysis and design stage compared to a bug fix request that requires only a brief or no analysis or design stage.

Add other workflow stages as appropriate to the project scenario, such as Backlog, To Do, Ready to Deploy, Done, and Blocked. Some of these should also have a WIP limit to improve the flow. These limits can be fine tuned based on experience.

Once the workflow stages are decided, create the columns on the board that represent the abstracted workflow stages. Various work items that go into two main cadences, Scrum and Kanban, are also defined as different cadences (horizontal rows).

Task Board

The task board is a good instrument for planned cadence part of the work where each Story has multiple tasks. In order not to crowd the Scrumban board, a separate task board can be used to track various tasks against each story. It is not mandatory to have a task board, but if not too much burden, it could be very valuable. The Scrumban board tracks the high level Work Request, and the Task board tracks the detailed tasks for each of those work requests.

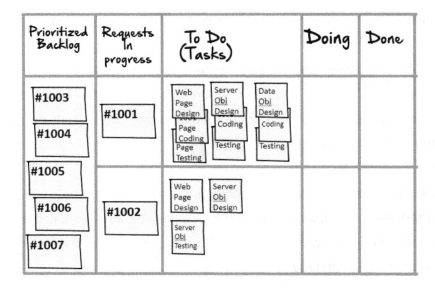

Prioritized Backlog	Requests In progress	To Do (Tasks)	Doing	Done
#1003 #1004	#1001	Web Page Design / Page Coding / Page Testing Server Obj Design / Coding / Testing Data Obj Design / Coding / Testing		
#1005 #1006 #1007	#1002	Web Page Design Server Obj Design Server Obj Testing		

Typical Scrumban task board

Each row on the task board is a user story (Work Request). In release planning meeting, the team selects the product backlog items they can complete in the next sprint. Every user story is turned into multiple tasks, and each of these is represented by one task card that is placed on the Task board.

Virtual Board

Agile Manifesto values individuals and interactions over processes and tools. The whole point of Scrumban is to track the flow of work visually on a physical board. This also facilitates good team communication during the daily stand ups and after meetings to gather around a physical board. A physical board is also advantageous as it forces people to be in the same room and communicate face-to-face. It is a known fact that 75-80% of communication is non-verbal, so nothing can replace the physical board and face-to-face interactions.

However, in today's scenario, it is a luxury to have a collocated team, as most of the teams are geographically distributed. You should be happy if all the team members are in the same time zone. There is also a good chance that one or more people could be working from home on any given day. Considering all these factors, having an electronic board would be very practical. It is a best practice to have both virtual as well as a physical board. For example, the team is distributed across two locations with each having more than one team member at a location. The team can maintain one Virtual board as the single source of truth, but also have two physical boards in each location.

The virtual board is where most of the updates happen, but the physical board in each location can be updated once or twice daily if it is not too much of an effort or overhead. The physical board has its own advantages such as visualize the flow of work, better understanding of the bottlenecks, clear visibility of the blocked items, impact of related work requests, and tasks.

Scrumban Cards

There are various types of cards in Scrumban model, they represent different functions and each follow specific color coding system to create a visual impact. Each Scrumban card carries important piece of information on it. The design of these cards can be customized as per the requirements of the project scenario. Some of the important ones are Work Request card, Defect Card, Issue Card and Task Card. Before we discuss some of the key aspects of these cards, following section describes the color coding system to be defined for these cards. This is just a sample color coding system, you can define your own system which suits your project requirement.

Card Colors

It is a best practice to use color coding for various types of cards to denote the significance of the work request type or task or any activity type. The main purpose of color coding system is to create a visual impact, to quickly identify the cards on the board. For example, a Red card on the board would immediately draw attention of the team that there is reported defect to be fixed in a particular work request. A purple card would make the team aware that there is a Fixed Date work item on the board. So, it is essential to define and follow a standard color coding system. Every team member should follow these standards while placing cards on the board to make this system effective.

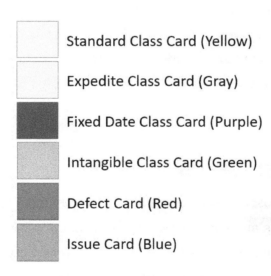

Standard Class Card (Yellow)

Expedite Class Card (Gray)

Fixed Date Class Card (Purple)

Intangible Class Card (Green)

Defect Card (Red)

Issue Card (Blue)

Sample Scrumban card colors

These colors could be based on various factors, for example class of service (Expedite, Standard, Intangible, Fixed Date), or work type (minor enhancement, bug fix, data fix). Some of the sample colors for various classes of services are shown in this image. There could be many configurations to make the system visually interactive.

Work Request Card

Every work request should have a card on the board. The Work Request card describes work request number, work description, work type, class of service, any special instructions, any dates and any other details that are essential. The information on the cards must facilitate the pull system and empower individuals to make their own pull decisions. Sometimes the format of the information on a card may vary by work item type or by class of service.

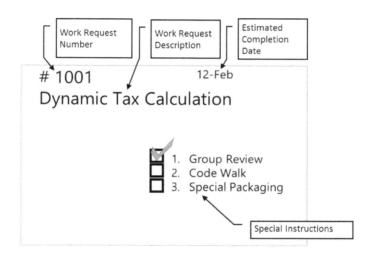

Example of Scrumban Work Request card

In the above example, the number in the top left is the work request number used to uniquely identify the item and to link it to the electronic version of the tracking system or the number that is given by the client or internal system of your organization. The work request description or name is written in the middle. Several dates can feature on this card depending on the requirement, for example, the creation date, estimated completion date, and the actual completion date. These dates could help in facilitating first-in-first-out (FIFO) queuing for the standard class of service, and it allows team members to see how many days have elapsed against the service level agreement. For fixed delivery date class-of-service items, the required delivery date is mentioned in a prominent place to visually show the delivery date.

Defect Card

It is also a good practice to have defect card created for any "critical" defect and keep it attached to the work request card. It is not recommended to create defect card for every defect that is being worked on, this could cause clutter on the board. This card should only be restricted to defects that have wider impact, a potential showstopper defect only qualifies for a defect ticket. The idea is to clearly identify any critical defects across the board at any moment.

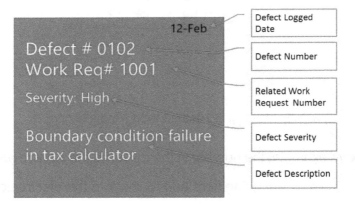

Example of Defect card

The card should be of a color that is clearly visible on the board, so Red color would be the most appropriate. The information on the defect card should be - logged date, defect number assigned in the defect tracking system, the work request it is possibly related, defect severity and a brief defect description.

As shown in the below illustration, it is important to post the defect card attached to the Work Request it is related to for immediate reference.

	Backlog	To Do	Analysis (3)		Build (5)		Test (2)		Ready	Deploy
			Doing	Done	Doing	Done	Doing	Done		
Scrumban										
	Backlog	To Do (5)	Analysis (3)		Build (5)		Test (2)		Ready	Deploy
			Doing	Done	Doing	Done	Doing	Done		
EXPEDITE										
STANDARD										
INTANGIBLE										

Illustration of Defect card on Visual board

These defect card would attract the attention of various team members to collaborate and resolve it quickly. Also Product Owner and Scrumban Master would be able to help in expediting the defect closure from the process perspective.

Issue Card

Another good practice is to have an issue card created for any "major" issue and keep it attached to the work request card. Avoid creating an issue card for every issue, it should only be limited to major issues which could potentially impact the timeline or any other important metric. This practice clearly identifies any major issues across the board.

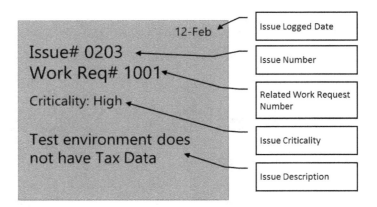

Example of Issue card

The card should be of a color that is clearly visible on the board, so blue color would be the most appropriate. The information on the issue card should be - logged date, issue number assigned in the issue tracking system, the work request it is possibly related, issue criticality and a brief issue description. As shown in the below illustration, it is important to post the issue card attached to the Work Request it is related to for immediate reference.

	Backlog	To Do	Analysis (3)		Build (5)		Test (2)		Ready	Deploy
			Doing	Done	Doing	Done	Doing	Done		
Scrumban										
	Backlog	To Do (5)	Analysis (3)		Build (5)		Test (2)		Ready	Deploy
			Doing	Done	Doing	Done	Doing	Done		
EXPEDITE										
STANDARD										
INTANGIBLE										

Illustration of Issue card on Visual board

140

More blue cards on the board means obstruction to the flow which should be resolved with high priority to restore the flow. This practice allows the Scrumban Master and team lead to visualize the road blocks in one glance and get down to help the team in resolving the issue.

Team Badges

The team badges are visual aids to identify each team member with their picture or name on them. It is to visually identify who is working on which work request or task, and at the same time limit the number of work requests being worked on at any point in time by each team member. There should be only one or two badges per person on the board. The only exception for this is when the team member's time is shared across different projects. But make sure the effort split across these projects is estimated and measured to avoid any overbooking of the member's time.

Example of Team Badges

These badges should be placed on the Work Requst card or Task card to visually represent the work allocation. It allows the team lead to visuallize the work allocations and helps in work load balancing.

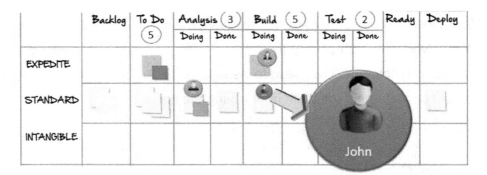

Illustration of Team Badges on the Visual board

These badges would help in controlling number of work requests or tasks per person by restricting a fixed number of badges allowed per person. For examples, there should be only two badges per person on the board which restricts the person to work on not more than two requests at a time. This maximum number of badges per person can be refined and made it as an unbreakable rule to make it effective.

These are the basic components of Scrumban system you need to implement as step three. There are many best practices that can be implemented to make your Scrumban more effective, avoid too many practices to keep it lean and agile. Start with these basic components, but experiment and make incremental changes as you go along your Scrumban journey.

Summary

1. Create Scrumban board – columns and rows based on the Step 1 and Step 2 sections.

2. Decide whether you need a task board. If yes, decide on the columns and rows and create the task board.

3. Decide on various Scrumban cards, e.g., work request card, task card, defect card, and issue card.

4. Standardize the color coding for various Scrumban cards.

5. Decide on the important information to be written on each of these cards and standardize this so that the team follows it consistently.

6. Create a team badge for each team member; decide if you need to have more than one badge for each team member. These badges should be placed on the Work Request or Task cards to visually represent the work allocations.

***

Chapter 11

Step 4 – Defining Team, Artifacts and Ceremonies

"Coming together is the beginning, keeping together is progress and working together is success." – Henry Ford

Scrumban structure consists of team structure, key artifacts, ceremonies, service level definitions, metrics, and charts. These are basic structural elements to implement Scrumban, and are not exhaustive or mandatory in anyway. These can be defined as appropriate for the project scenario.

Team structure

Software Maintenance teams are structured in various different permutations and combinations based on the workload distribution, work in-flow fluctuations or contractual or budgetary constraints. Ideally, it should be one common team that works across all work types – enhancements and non-enhancements, or planned work and unplanned work, however there are various other possibilities depending on what suits the project the best. The most common options to form your teams are discussed below for reference purpose.

A common team would have all the team members working without any silos in between, team needs to follow well-defined guidelines in pulling the work in to work-in-progress. The capacity or effort utilized across these two cadences can be dynamically adjusted to some extent without causing any disruption to the flow. This may require extra management bandwidth to maintain an efficient work flow.

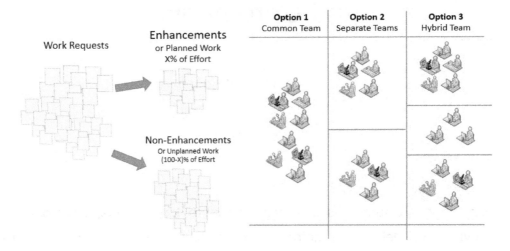

Various possibilities of team structure

The option of separate teams would have two separate teams focused on planned and unplanned work cadences to ensure that flow rate across. The downside to this model is that any fluctuations in the work inflow rate may not get handled effectively.

A hybrid team with two separate teams with a small team in a common pool in between would handle the work inflow fluctuations better.

Roles

Scrumban focuses more on the importance of team interactions than following any process. Deciding on the team structure is an essential and ever-evolving process step. Should it be a cross-functional team? Should it be a specialist team? The answer is that it should be a combination of both, as some part of work is managed by a cross-functional team and the other part of work is managed by specialist teams. A combined team is what is needed to implement Scrumban. The Scrumban Master and Product Owner are the other essential roles to implement this model. Some of the standard roles are defined below as a guidance. These can be customized as appropriate.

Product Owner or Portfolio Owner (PO)

The Product Owners one of the two most pivotal roles in Scrumban, this role represents business or end user community to provide guidance to the team, and provides a generalized view of the requirements and expectations. Product Owner owns the backlog by representing the interests of all the stakeholders and ensures the work delivered meets those needs.

It is normally one person who acts as a Product Owner. There could be some scenarios where it is very difficult to identify one person. In such scenarios, it is advisable to have one person who represents all the other Product Owners. This situation arises when there is a portfolio of business applications or software products that the team is maintaining. Whatever the scenario may be, it is very essential to have one person play the primary Product Owner role. The responsibilities of the Product Owner are:

As an owner

1. Owning the backlog is one of the primary responsibilities of the Product Owner, and this is an on-going job and a full-time activity.

2. Prioritization of backlog: With the help of stakeholders or sometimes with inputs from the team, keeping the backlog up to date with the priorities of each item. The Product Owner is required to have the Backlog sequenced prior to the Sprint Planning Meeting for the planned work cadence. On the unplanned cadence, making sure the automatic prioritization methods are all in place, and monitor and refine as appropriate.

3. Grooming: Facilitating the elicitation process of Epics, Themes, and Features into user stories that are granular enough to be achieved in a single sprint. User Stories are elaborated at the last moment possible and it is the Product Owner's responsibility to be there during the Sprint Planning meeting to help the teams understand exactly what is required.

As a business representative

1. Conveys the Vision and Goals at the beginning of every Release and Sprint. The Product Owner must continuously remind the Team of the Sprint and Release goals. This helps keep the team on track and serves as an over-arching yardstick for the team to measure their activity and progress.

2. Representing the stakeholders: The Product Owner must continuously engage the users and stakeholders to ensure the team is building the

right software changes, and therefore delivering the return on investment expected of it.

3. Participation in the Scrumban process: Product Owner should participate in the daily Stand-up meetings, planning meetings, sprint reviews, and retrospectives.

As an administrator

1. Inspects the progress at the end of every Sprint and has complete authority to accept or reject work done. Work that is either incomplete or not done needs to be reprioritized or sequenced.

2. Communicates status externally. The Product Owner is the voice of the Team to the outside world and should ensure that all channels of communications are open and that projects have the right amount of support required to succeed.

3. Terminates a Sprint if it is determined that a drastic change in direction is required.

Scrumban Master

The second most pivotal role in Scrumban. Some call this role Scrumban Sensei. In this publication, it is referred as Scrumban Master for convenience. The Scrumban Master is a servant leader, a facilitator, and a mentor who ensures that the Scrumban practices are followed to deliver the best output from the team. The Scrumban master plays 3 roles in the Scrumban process, as follows.

Process Owner

1. Responsible for making sure the team lives by the values and practices of Scrumban.

2. Ensures that practices are adhered to by all the stakeholders. This involves Product Owner maintaining the backlog, conducting all the meetings in the most effective way, maintaining all the artifacts in a disciplined manner, updating metrics and charts, and reporting and monitoring on a regular basis.

3. Improves the professional lives of the team members by facilitating creativity and empowerment.

4. Improves the productivity of the team by ensuring Scrumban is understood and enacted.

Problem Solver

1. Identifies impediments the team is facing, facilitates meetings to resolve the impediments, and makes sure the work is not impacted.

2. Manages the Impediments Log to run the process with fewer interruptions.

As a Protector

1. Acts as a protector of the team. The most common example is that the Scrumban Master protects the team by making sure they do not over-commit themselves to what they can achieve during a sprint due to pressure from an overly aggressive Product Owner.

2. Ensures the team does not get complacent.

Team

The team has to be a combination of both cross functional team members and specialist team members. Across functional group of people is responsible for delivering the potential shippable increments on the Planned Work cadence.

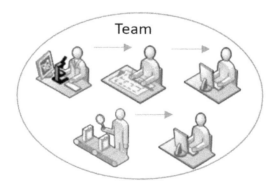

On the Unplanned Work cadence, there could be multiple functional groups participating to fulfill certain specialist tasks. In cases where these groups are not part of the dedicated team, they have to be managed with a certain commitment on the bandwidth to be dedicated towards the Software Maintenance team. Sometimes, you may have to define OLAs (Operation

Level Agreements) or UCs (Underpinning Contracts) with these specialized groups for the groups to respond and complete these specialized services.

Artifacts

Less effort to be spent on documentation or maintaining artifacts, so it is advised to use a minimal number of artifacts.

Backlog

The backlog is a list of Work Requests of a software or a group of software. These Work Requests could range from a large enhancement to a small bug fix. The backlog should contain details of the work requests such as software product name, change description, requester, business priority, technical complexity, business impact, Order of Magnitude, Estimate, Planned Release number, and Planned Sprint number.

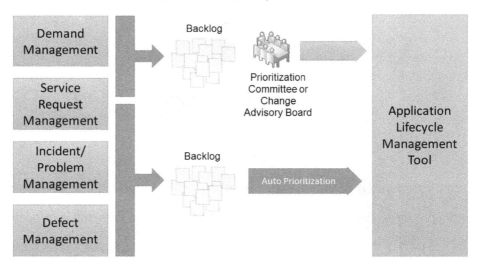

Backlog formation

Each work request in the backlog typically refers to a Demand Order (or

Change Order) from the Demand Management system or a defect from the Defect Management system, or an incident from the Incident Management system, or Service Request from the Service Request Management system. It varies from organization to organization. It depends on how and from where all these Work Requests are stored and tracked is very specific to a project scenario. The best way to implement this would be to integrate the work requests source systems with any standard Agile tool to avoid manual effort in managing the Backlog.

Prioritized Backlog

The Prioritized Backlog is an ordered backlog with priorities set for each Work Request. As soon as capacity is available, the Work Requests from the top of the product backlog will be picked up by the team to start the work.

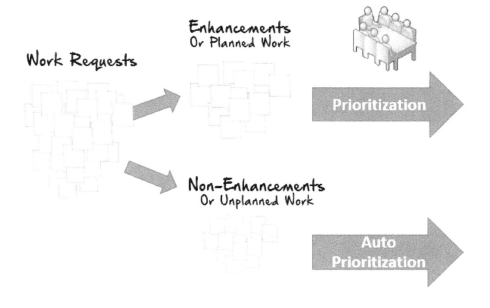

Prioritization process

Planned Work cadence: Anyone in the team can edit the Planned Work (Enhancements) backlog, but the Product Owner is ultimately responsible for ordering the work requests in the backlog based on inputs from the business, users, or stakeholders.

Unplanned Work cadence: The Unplanned Work (Non-enhancement) requests flow is more dynamic in nature; the work items typically flow from an ITSM (IT Service Management) tool or any standard Software Support Management tool. These would mostly be service requests, bug fixes, user queries, and these are typically associated with a ticket number, details, priority, and other attributes. The order should be decided based on a set of rules or policies defined at the tool level to determine the order of the backlog. Product Owner will be able to override the preset order given by the tool to meet any additional priorities of the stakeholders.

Parking lot or Blocked Items:

The parking lot or Blocked item list is for staging the Work Requests or tasks that the team cannot finish due to an external dependency or impediment. Instead of keeping it in its current stage, it is moved to the Parking Lot and kept there until the impediment is resolved. An example would be if a special environment needed to test the software change is getting delayed; this would prevent the Work Request from progressing.

Backlog	To Do	Doing	Done	Deploy	Blocked

Blocked items

Placing an item in the parking lot prevents the team from deadlocks, where unfinished items block the flow. The Blocked Items are kept in a separate column on the Card Wall. This provides good visibility of all blocked items. The information should also be plotted on the Cumulative Flow Diagram for better visibility, and a root-cause analysis should be conducted to avoid such road blocks in future.

Scrumban Master and Team Lead must focus on this column and restrict the number of cards in this column. Without actively working in resolving the Blocked Items results in work getting piled up and impacts the flow efficiency. This is one metric that should be highlighted so that it gets enough attention, managing this to a lowest number would deliver great results.

Impediments List

In Scrumban, it is mandatory to maintain an Impediments List for tracking and monitoring all the impediments that team faces on a day to day basis. An impediment is an issue that is obstructing the team from moving forward or slowing down the velocity. These could be related to knowledge gaps, technical issues, Scrumban adoption issues, process issues, and business- or customer-related issues.

It is one of the primary responsibilities of the Scrumban Master to track, monitor, and resolve these impediments. The team reports these impediments immediately to the Scrumban Master in the Daily Stand-up meeting. They are logged into the Impediment List, and Scrumban Master works with the concerned team members or stakeholders in facilitating their resolution at the earliest possible time.

Ceremonies

Ceremonies are events or meetings in Scrumban to achieve certain important objectives of the model. The list of meetings and the way they are conducted may vary depending on the project scenario. A few important ceremonies are described below. Though there is no sprint concept in Unplanned Work cadence, to align to a certain frequency it is recommended to take Sprint Duration (from the Planned Work Cadence) as the unit scale to define the ceremonies or duration between release to release.

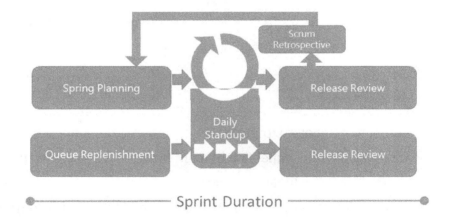

Scrumban Ceremonies

In a typical Sprint Duration, the team should have one Sprint Planning, one Release Review, one Scrum Retrospective, and multiple Daily Stand-up meetings. On Unplanned Work cadence, team should have one Queue Replenishment, Release Review for each release, and multiple Daily Stand-up meetings.

To keep the number of meetings to an optimum, it is suggested to combine Sprint Planning and Queue Replenishment to bring in more synergy across Planned Work and Unplanned work cadences. It is also prudent to have a common Daily Stand-up for Unplanned Work cadence and combine it, though it is not a common practice in pure Kanban implementation. Also consider having a separate Release Review for the Unplanned Work cadence to identify any continuous improvement opportunities that may increase the effectiveness of the model and the team as well.

Sprint Planning

Sprint Planning is for deciding on the scope of the Sprint and committing to a plan for delivering work requests. This activity is applicable to the Planned Work cadence and its ceremony happens at the beginning of every Sprint to move the Work Requests from the Prioritized Backlog into the current Sprint backlog.

Objective	To finalize Sprint cadence scope and plan the iteration
Frequency	Once in delivery cadence duration
Moderator	Product Owner
Prerequisites	A prioritized backlog approved by the Product Owner. Team capabilities and velocity. High-level vision and business objectives
Roles & Responsibilities	Scrumban Master: Facilitates the meeting.
	Product Owner: Represents a general view of the business objectives in prioritizing the backlog.

| | Team: Provides insights into technical feasibility, estimates, and dependencies. Pull the work requests from Backlog to Sprint Backlog. |
| | Stakeholders: Advises the team as decisions are made around the sprint planning. |

Queue Replenishment

This may not be needed in case the automatic replenishment is set up. In such cases, the work gets prioritized based on the policies defined and gets moved into To-Do column for the team to pick.

The Queue Replenishment is a ceremony to prioritize the work items. Frequency is based on a need to replenish the queue, depending on the input cadence, but needs to happen often to keep the optimal number of items in the To-Do queue. The participants include Scrumban Master, Product Owners, and other relevant business representatives.

Objective	To plan the backlog for the Unplanned Work cadence
Frequency	Depends on the availability of the work request left in the To-Do column
Moderator	Product Owner
Prerequisites	Predefined policies to be used for prioritization
Roles & Responsibilities	Scrumban Master: Facilitates the meeting.
	Product Owner: Represents a general view of the product backlog.
	Team: Provides insight into technical feasibility

	and dependencies.
	Stakeholders: Acts as trusted advisors when decisions are made around the release plan.

Daily Stand-up

One of the most important features of this model is the Daily Stand-up meeting. This meeting ensures that Scrumban Master and the team members are in sync with the happenings across the project. Every day, the team gathers together, usually in a team room or private office—to report on the progress made since the last meeting, goals for the next one, and any impediments blocking their path. It is a short, time-boxed meeting, no more than 15 minutes in duration. It should take place every day at the same time, preferably the first thing in the morning before the team starts work. Each team member answers three questions and the Scrumban Master identifies ways to resolve impediments.

1. What have I done since yesterday?

2. What am I planning to do today?

3. What are my impediments?

If any issue cannot be covered in the limited amount of time, Scrumban Master or a team member would organize a "sidebar" meeting just after the Daily Stand-up. This would make the Daily Stand-up effective and efficient, without wasting other team members' time. It is often seen that teams spend more than 15 minutes. You can apply this strategy to stick to the timeline. Some of the practices are to use of stop watches, avoiding distracting small talks, or a talking stick or mascot (a team member must hold it up to speak in the meeting).

Objective	To plan the downstream delivery
Frequency	Once every working day
Moderator	Scrumban Master
Prerequisites	Updated Scrumban board
Roles & Responsibilities	Scrumban Master: Identifies impediments. Records, tracks, and resolves impediments. Instructs and facilitates Sidebar meetings for topics that are confined to a subset of team members.
	Team: Each team member answers 3 questions.

Release Review

In Planned Work cadence, when the sprint ends it is time for the team to present its work to the Product Owner. This meeting is called Release Review meeting. The team demonstrates a potentially shippable product increment developed during the sprint. The Product Owner reviews the deliverables and decides which work requests are truly done.

Objective	To plan the downstream delivery
Frequency	Once in delivery cadence duration
Moderator	Product Owner
Prerequisites	Finished work requests
Roles & Responsibilities	Scrumban Master: Facilitates the meeting.
	Product Owner: Reviews, accepts or rejects the work requests.

	Team: Demo the finished work requests.
	Stakeholders: Reviews, accepts, or rejects the work requests.

Retrospective

The Scrumban Master holds the retrospective to reflect on the past production cycle in order to ensure continuous process improvements. This happens after every Release Review meeting. The Scrumban Master asks two questions in the Retrospective meeting:

1. What went well during the last cycle?

2. What should improve in the next cycle?

The focus of this meeting is to identify what went well, what didn't, and what improvements could be made in the next sprint. Team members should be encouraged to speak frankly about the sprint's successes and failures. It is an especially important opportunity for the team to focus on its effectiveness and identify strategies to improve its processes. The retrospective allows the Scrumban Master to observe and identify common impediments that impact the team.

Objective	To identify improvement opportunities based on what went right and what went wrong
Frequency	End of sprint or Release Window
Moderator	Product Owner

Prerequisites	Impediments list
	Blocked Items
	Release Review comments
Roles & Responsibilities	Scrumban Master: Facilitates the meeting with open and honest feedback. Ensures participation from all the team members.
	Product Owner: Represents the stakeholder's feedback.
	Team: Focuses on receiving as much feedback as possible with specific details.
	Stakeholders: Provides feedback to improve the process.

Team identifies the root cause or resolutions behind the impediments and comes up with action items to improve the practices in the next iteration. These action items are reviewed on a continuous basis to ensure the effectiveness of the Retrospectives.

After meetings or Sidebar Meetings

The Scrumban Master organizes "After Meetings" (also called as Sidebar meetings) whenever there is a problem in the flow. For example, a story is over the expected cycle time, or a task is frequently re-assigned and not yet solved. Both the development team and Product Owner participate in this meeting and work on a solution to solve the open issue. These meetings are typically offshoots of the Daily Stand-up meeting, mostly around the impediments reported which demand meetings among the respective team members.

Issue Log review

The team uses this meeting to review the issues and identifies the action items to resolve the issue. The frequency of this meeting depends on the scenario, but it should happen regularly to resolve issues to improve the workflow. In certain situations, issues need to be escalated to get the resolutions from other groups. Scrumban Master is responsible to take action to escalate issues to the concerned group for resolution. It is important to have clear escalation paths and policies to make it effective.

These are the basic roles, artifacts and ceremonies to be implemented, however you customize these to suit to your project scenario.

Summary

1. Consider existing team structure, roles, artifacts, and ceremonies while deicding on the new roles, artifacts, and ceremonies.

2. Define team roles and their responsibilities, have training and orientation sessions to enable individuals and team to align with the new structure.

3. Define the artifacts, have the templates and tools ready to align with the new structure.

4. Define the ceremonies, have training and orientation sessions to enable team to align with the new structure.

***

Chapter 12

Step 5 - Setting Metrics & Charts

"Not everything that counts can be counted, and
not everything that can be counted counts." –
Albert Einstein

It is often said that "What gets measured gets done." Measurements and Metrics describe the purpose and priorities of a process or a model. Time and resources devoted to measurement demonstrate team's commitment that the object of the measurement is important. Therefore, the selection of appropriate metrics is an essential starting point for process improvement.

There are numerous metrics and charts that teams already use in Software Maintenance: Productivity, Defect Injection Rate, Cost of Quality, Schedule Adherence, and Effort Variance. Adding more metrics increases load on the team and slows them down. So it is very essential to review all the metrics and charts in place, and assess the effort spent vs value derived, in order to identify which can be dropped to optimize the load on the team. Some of the most essential metrics and charts are discussed below. Implement the ones that are relevant to your scenario. Most of the tools available in the market to manage Scrum and Kanban would have these metrics and charts built-in already, otherwise, measure and track such metrics manually.

Metrics

To execute any repetitive set of activities to achieve desired or better results every time, a well-defined process is required. Every process needs to be measured to assess performance and also to improve the process and achieve intended results. It is essential to define what needs to be measured and improved; and this definition will lead to the identification of a measurement, or metric.

Lead Time & Cycle Time

The Lead Time is the time between the moment change request is raised (typically by the user) and the moment it is delivered back to the requester. Lead Time is what the user experiences from the time a change is requested and the time it is ready to use. The Cycle Time is the time between the moment software maintenance team picks up the work request to start the work and the request is ready for delivery.

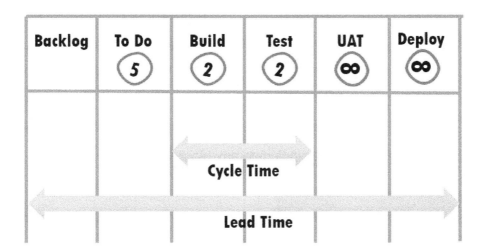

Lead Time and Cycle Time metrics

Cycle Time is more of an engineering measurement of the team's capability. The Cycle Time is what is measured normally by Software Maintenance teams, but Lead Time is a must have metric in Scrumban. Measuring Cycle Time helps in understanding the waste in the end to end lifecycle. Since Lead Time is what user experiences, it is the true measure of the end to end process efficiency.

It is very important to measure both Cycle Time and Lead Time for all the work requests. Whether it is planned cadence or unplanned cadence, these two metrics would help in identifying the root cause for inefficiencies and finding solutions for better efficiency.

Flow Efficiency

The Flow Efficiency is a ratio of actual working time or Cycle Time and end to end Lead Time.

The calculation of flow efficiency is as follows:

Flow Efficiency in % = Actual Cycle Time / Actual Lead Time
- Where, Actual Cycle Time = Time spent by a Request in the in-progress stages
- Lead Time = Time elapsed between Request moved in to Backlog and ready to deploy including any blocked time.

Flow Efficiency is a very useful metric to identify the improvements in reducing the lead time on a continuous basis.

Throughput

Throughput is nothing but "Velocity" of the Unplanned Work cadence. It is a measurement of how much work the team gets done in a specified duration of time (typically in a week). Throughput is what actually got done in a specific duration and not what is planned. It is typically measured in work requests or tickets or any measure that suits the work that gets delivered. This measurement is applicable to the Unplanned Work cadence of Scrumban. This metric can be plotted as the trend to see how this can be increased on a continuous basis.

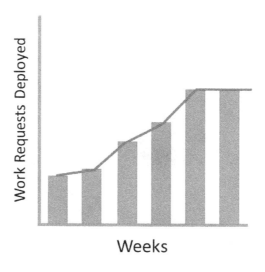

Throughput metric

A best practice is to report throughput in terms of number of items completed in a unit time (week or two weeks or a month). It is only applicable for non-time boxed part of the work. The goal is to provide visibility into the throughput and improve it on a continuous basis. The unit of the work should be consistent or else this would give a wrong picture of the progress.

Blocked Work Items

This is a simple set of metric to measure the number of issues and blocked items on a daily basis. This is a very important metric which could potentially help in solving lot of flow efficiency issues. Monitoring this metric would help in understanding how well the blocked items are logged, monitored, and resolved.

This chart should be monitored every day and appropriate actions should be taken, including escalating it to the higher levels as appropriate.

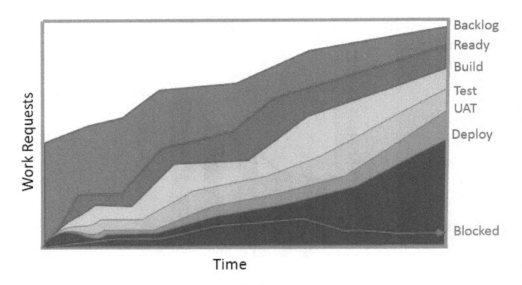

Blocked items

The blocked work items metric helps the team in analyzing the common reasons for the blocking of the work items. Pareto analysis should be conducted to identify continuous improvement opportunities, and corrective actions should be implemented to reduce the number of blocked items in future. This analysis can be conducted during the Retrospectives or any regular frequency.

The key to an effective use of this metric is to ensure that a reason code is assigned to each blocked work request and the time lost on each blocking reason code. However, data gathering and blocked work analysis is not easy to do without a good tool. It would be tedious to do it manually. Identify a tool that has good features to analyze the blocked item root causes.

Due Date Performance

For Fixed Date Class work items, measuring the due date performance is a must. This would give a sense of how the team is performing on this important metric. This would help in fine tuning the cadence level WIP or any other impediment causing this performance metric to slip.

Velocity

Velocity is derived metric based on the work delivered based on the past iterations. Velocity is an average work delivered per iteration, not what is planned. In Scrumban, like any typical scrum velocity, it is measured in Story Points. A story depending on its complexity is given certain story points, if the team does 5 stories that are 6 story points each in one iteration, the team's velocity is 30 story points. This measurement is applicable to the planned cadence of Scrumban.

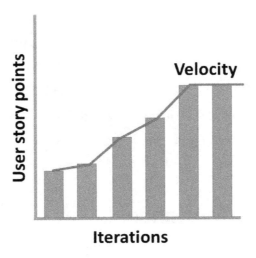

Velocity metric

Few clarifications on the definition of Velocity:

- Velocity is the sum of the delivered work per iteration. It should be measured in the same units used for estimation of the work – mostly in story points not in the units of effort or tasks.

- Velocity is a measurement made after the fact, and is used to plan ahead.

- Only aggregate velocity of the team should be measured, individual velocity is not a good measure.

- Comparison of Velocity among different teams may not give the right picture for the simple reason that different teams may have different estimation approaches. However, it is possible if they all use the same estimation approach.

Initially, in the first few iterations, it is a good practice to plan a Velocity assuming 40% of the available capacity of the team. This is to account for the learning curve, meetings, email, documentation, unplanned rework, collaboration, research, and so on. For example, 10 programmers and 2 week iterations amounts to 100 person days of capacity. The planned Velocity should be assuming 40 person days of work per iteration to factor in the other considerations mentioned above.

Typically, it takes 3 iterations to stabilize any team to deliver consistent velocity, and no more than 6. Velocity fluctuations within a reasonable range are common, but if the fluctuations are very wide and continue for more than one or two iterations, it is necessary to re-estimate and negotiate the release plans.

Velocity depends on keeping the team consistent. In Scrumban it is necessary to alter the team size while stabilizing the planned and unplanned cadences, or while the business is shifting gears and the work that is flowing into planned and unplanned cadences is changing. Increase or reduce planned velocity as suits the business and project scenario. Any change would take one or two iterations to understand the new velocity.

One important aspect of velocity is to view this metric in conjunction with other measurements and activities. High velocity does not mean the team is productive in delivering quality. Velocity should be seen in combination with the number of defects, unit testing time, amount of customer collaborations, and the amount of rework. Strike a balance across all the other factors, while estimating the Velocity that is ideal for the team during the spring planning.

Charts

Scrumban needs at least two charts to reflect the current status of the work:

Burn-down chart and Cumulative Flow Diagram. These charts should be maintained on a near real time basis, and also must be displayed in places where everyone in the team can see every day.

Cumulative Flow Diagram (CFD)

A cumulative flow diagram is a Chart used in queuing theory. It is an area graph that depicts the quantity of work in a given state, showing arrivals, time in queue, quantity in queue, and departure. In Scrumban, it helps visually represent the performance of the Unplanned Work cadence, but depending on how you implement Scrumban, this can be used for Planned cadence as well.

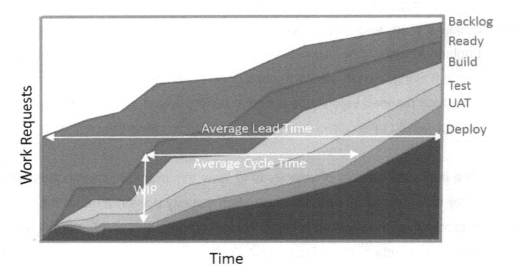

Cumulative Flow Diagram

A big part of the cumulative flow diagram is its ability to visualize the WIP, cycle times, and lead times, which help in identifying bottlenecks or wastage in the flow. It is a very powerful and descriptive tool, and should be displayed in a place where all the team members can view it and update it on a daily basis.

The CFD primarily used for tracking and forecasting the completion of work requests, and throws lights upon areas which need process improvement.

The CFD is a graphical representation of how the work is flowing through the Scrumban system, helps in stabilizing the flow, focuses upon bottlenecks. It depicts the work in progress (WIP), entry rate, exit rate, lead time, throughput, cycle time and other important measurements.

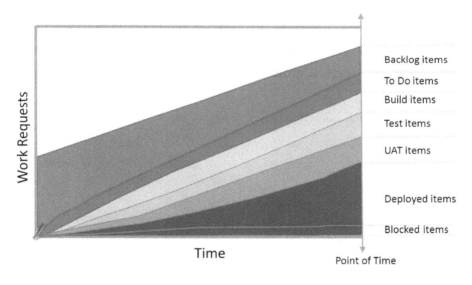

Point of time view

The diagram shows the number of work items or tasks in each stage of the process at a "point of time". Different colors represent tasks in different columns on the chart. The red and maroon areas show tasks that need to be done, the yellow and light green areas show work in progress, and the dark green area represents all the finished tasks.

The most important ones to watch are the yellow and light green areas. If these increase or widen vertically with time, it means that there are problems or bottlenecks and the Lead Time will probably be increased.

Any sudden change within any band of tasks would indicate that there is an issue with the flow. From successive accumulation of tasks in a certain band, you can also foresee bottlenecks, and by this make an effort to try and eliminate the bottlenecks. This diagram also visually shows the average Lead Time, average cycle time, and WIP at any instance.

As shown in the figure below, the ideal flow of the work request in various stages should be evenly flowing, with bands staying almost even, except for the "Deploy" band, which should be continuously getting taller, as the number of requests done is growing constantly.

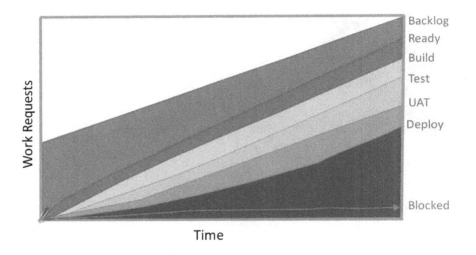

Cumulative Flow diagram – Ideal flow

This is some basic information about CFD, there is lot to learn about how to effectively use it to measure entry rate, exit rate, burn-up rate, Average Lead Time, and WIP to make necessary changes to the process to make the system efficient.

Burn-down chart

A burn down chart is a graphical representation of remaining effort versus time. This chart provides a single planning and tracking tool for the Planned Work cadence of Scrumban, but depending on how you implement Scrumban, this may not be required to implement.

This chart gets reset for every iteration with the new set of effort, story points, or tasks of the iteration. The effort (or backlog) or Story Points or Tasks are often on the vertical axis, with Time along the horizontal axis.

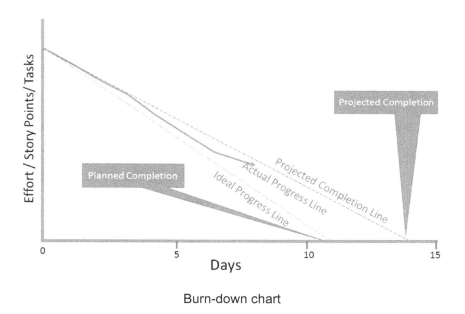

Burn-down chart

The chart has three primary lines:

- "Ideal Progress Line," formed by joining the total effort point on the Y axis and planned completion date on the X axis.

- "Actual Progress Line," formed by joining all the points formed by the remaining effort on the Y axis and the day of the reading on the X axis.

- "Projected Completion Line," formed by joining the total effort point on Y axis, latest point of the "Actual Progress Line," and extending this to intersect the X axis. The point at which this line touches the X axis is the Projected Completion day.

The sprint burn down chart is a publicly displayed chart showing remaining work in the sprint backlog. It is updated every day with the remaining work to be completed. It gives a simple view of the sprint progress in terms of the work to be completed.

Team owns the chart

The best part about the chart is that the team owns the scope of work and updates the estimated effort and remaining effort. This creates a sense ownership in the team to own the plan. As the team reviews and updates the chart, the team knows whether it is on track to meet the commitment or not. The team then becomes self-organized to stay on track and performs to expectation.

Single view of the scope

This chart represents one single view of the scope of the sprint. Anything that is not part of this chart is not in the scope of the sprint. The team plans what it has to accomplish in a sprint and updates the task list.

Daily visibility

In traditional project management, Schedule Variance and Effort Variance get tracked on a weekly or monthly basis, but the burn-down chart provides daily visibility. It helps in early mitigation of any risks. The planned line (green) and the projected line (red) provide the deviations clearly for the team to strategize the course correction steps.

Transparent reporting to all the stakeholders

A burn-down chart is a transparent reporting mechanism for the customer, stakeholders, and the team members. Typically, it is an online burn-down chart for all the stakeholders to view the status anywhere and anytime. In the absence of the online tool, team could paste a print-out or draw on the wall in the team's area.

How to set up and maintain a Burn-Down Chart?

All the Agile tools have burn-down charts built in. It can also be maintained in a Microsoft Excel spreadsheet.

1. The Time (number of days of the sprint) is plotted on the X axis, while remaining efforts / story points / tasks are plotted on the Y axis. The first step is to plot the Ideal Progress line, by joining total effort / story points as the first point on the Y axis, and the planned completion date on the X axis as the second point. This information is available after the breakdown activity, which is generally performed during the first Scrum planning meeting.

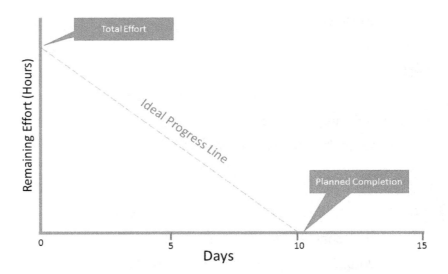

2. As the sprint progresses, the remaining effort should be plotted on the chart to show the progress line tending towards the planned completion point on the X axis.

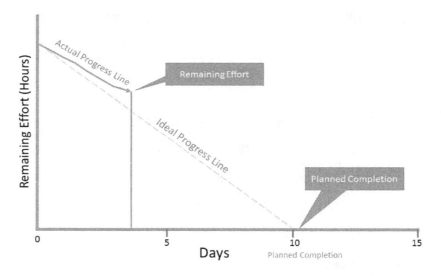

3. Draw the projected completion date based on the Actual Progress Line to estimate the actual completion.

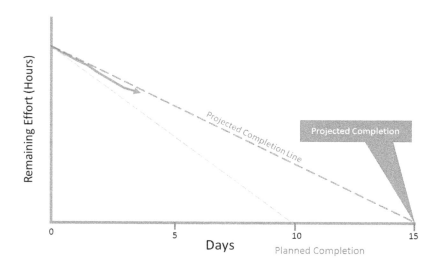

These are the basic metrics and charts that can be considered for implementation, but the key is to keep them simple and as minimal as possible. Implement automated tools to record, measure and report the metrics and charts in order to avoid the additional effort on the team.

Summary

1. Set up measurements and metrics relevant to your scenario viz. Velocity, Lead Time, Throughput, Flow Efficiency, Due Date Performance, and blocked items.

2. Set up control charts viz. Burndown Chart and Cumulative Flow Diagram.

***

Chapter 13

Journey forward

"If we know exactly where we're going, exactly how to get there, and exactly what we'll see along the way, we won't learn anything." – M. Scott Peck

Every Software Maintenance scenario is unique, and setting up Scrumban for your organization or project is going to be a unique journey. During this journey, you may have to make alterations to the model to suit to your requirements, or you may have to make changes to the way your teams function. Make these alterations to the controls, practices, or roles without losing the effectiveness of what Scrumban has to offer. Once you internalize this model, it becomes part of your organization or project. This step to internalize it is very important and needs a proper amount of planning.

In this chapter, we are going to discuss various aspects of a Scrumban journey that need to be focused on in order to make your journey successful.

Scrumban is also perceived as an efficient ecosystem to deliver Software Development and Maintenance. It is based on enforcement of simple constraints that will cause the team to self-organize into a highly efficient state. As it is based on complex adaptive systems theory, the teams have be self-organizing. A self-organizing team is a team that has highly motivated individuals who work together towards a common goal, with the ability and authority to take decisions, with the adaptability to respond to changing demands, and with a greater sense of ownership and commitment.

The work is pulled but not assigned. It is delivered as a group outcome, and the team is mentored and coached, not commanded or monitored. Self-organizing teams need to be "Competent" to deliver with less direction from others, they need to be "Collaborative" to function as a group not individuals, they need to be "Enthusiastic" to encourage and enthuse each other, and they need to have "Mutual trust and respect" to believe in each other's abilities and help each other in resolving issues.

Organization Change Management focus areas

The main point here is that it is not just a framework, it is setting up this ecosystem of process, technology, and people to make Scrumban journey successful.

Setting up and running Scrumban based on defined principles and practices is the primary objective of this journey, but later part of the journey is all about how to align with the goals and objectives set forth in the first place. All said and done, it is a huge organizational shift, and any change of this nature needs meticulous planning and implementation of activities that go beyond the model itself. Some of the main areas that need to be focused on are discussed below. This section is not exhaustive, so you may refer to your organization's specific change management process frameworks.

Vision, Mission and Value

Although I agree with the above quote from M. Scott Peck, there is also nothing like having a clear vision of the end state and a well thought-out mission to begin the journey. It is essential to have certain questions asked and answered to be clear about the purpose and the path of this Scrumban journey.

Vision & Mission chart

It helps in articulating the vision to all the stakeholders and keeping them on course. One of the critical success factors of Scrumban implementation is the alignment of vision and mission with all the stakeholders who will use the model day-in day-out. The articulation to the stakeholders has to be precise on why this change, how it helps and what changes need to be implemented.

Why change to Scrumban?

Most of the time organizations don't articulate why this change is needed in the first place. It leaves the stakeholders assuming that it is done for the benefit of the organization alone, which leads to misalignment within the mission. Scrumban is a model to help the teams and make it easy for them to deliver higher output with less effort. It delivers greater value to the organizations. The organization should have a clear vision and mission of Scrumban implementation that is communicated to all the stakeholders.

More importantly, there is the value that it can bring to the teams. This model should attract teams to adapt on their own rather than being pushed as another organizational level best practice. So articulating the value is most important.

How does Scrumban help?

Once it is established why the change is needed, stakeholders should be informed as to how the change will help them achieve their interests. This is both in terms of how Scrumban principles and practices would help improve average Lead Times, Flow Efficiency, or any other metric.

What is changing?

It is essential to define what is changing in terms of principles and practices in context of what is already in existence. Why are you doing what you are doing? What needs to be implemented to achieve it? Stakeholders would benefit from a big picture of the framework, practices, procedures, rollout plans, trainings, and supporting forums. This provides clarity for all the stakeholders, and helps them align better with the journey.

All these details need to be transformed in to artifacts which get fed through the organization communication channels – portals, blogs, communities, discussion forums, posters and emails. Having a vision and mission is not good enough. Good branding and socializing platform is a must in order to percolate these messages down to the grass root level.

Branding & Socializing

Scrumban branding should be clear on what Scrumban is, why it exists, what value it delivers, how it would make a difference to Software Maintenance stakeholders. Scrumban branding is a promise to deliver expected results, a promise that is conveyed through various organizational channels.

There is nothing like having an attractive logo, catchy brand name and apt tag line to start branding Scrumban in your organization. The branding should be easy to remember and should have certain "cool" factor associated with it so that programmer communities look forward to get associated with the brand. It is a good idea to involve a corporate design to make it more professional. This would also ensure that branding adhere to the corporate policies, guidelines, and formats.

Scrumban is a major shift in paradigm for Software teams. It requires a good amount of effort to be spent on socializing the vision, mission, "why, how and what" aspects of Scrumban to reinforce the need for Scrumban and its benefits to teams and stakeholders. This should happen through multiple avenues available within your organization such as newsletters, emails, leadership blogs, roadshows, organizational social networking portals, contests, and quizzes.

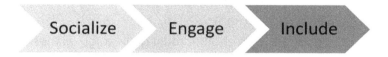

Branding tenets

Scrumban branding should be viewed as having three primary tenets. First tenet is "Socialize". In this phase the brand should be socialized with the programmer community. All the aspects of Scrumban brand – vision, mission, value, logo, and tagline should be spread through innovative channels, if not through traditional ones, such as emails, expert talks, or blogs. Once the brand is established and enough interest is generated in the programmer community, the second tenet of "Engage" should be triggered through roadshows, seminars, workshops, and quizzes. The third tenet "Include" is the most important, it takes the engagement levels higher by including the community to participate in customizing processes and practices, and identifying suitable measurements and metrics.

Enablement

Set up a good enablement framework for the team and other stakeholders. It should consist of four phases – Pre-Enablement, Enablement and Post-

Enablement with a Continuous Improvement phase.

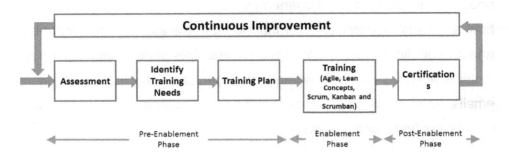

Enablement cycle

Every team member and stakeholder must go through all these four phases on a continuous basis.

Pre-Enablement phase

Every team member should be assessed on the process and tools knowledge required to be a part of the Scrumban project. Training needs should be identified accordingly, and a training plan should be created. The assessment should be done for each team member, as some of them may be already working on Scrum or Kanban projects. To avoid any duplication of effort in enablement of the teams, the assessment and training needs identification would help in creating an optimal training plan.

Enablement phase

The trainings should be conducted as per the training plan. Some of these trainings are specific to the role an individual is going to play in the team. Product Owner training should be different from team member's trainings.

Post Enablement phase

This is not a mandatory step for all the team members, but it is recommended to get certified to complete the enablement. These could be industry standard certifications or organizational certifications.

Continuous Improvement phase

At a certain frequency, whether semi-annual or annual, all team members should go through assessment in order to identify additional training needs and facilitate updates to the training plans.

Pilot & Rollout

Apart from having a good OCM team, four forces are essential for a successful Scrumban implementation, a dedicated Center of Excellence, Management support, Executive sponsorship, and programmer community. Ensure that Scrumban Center of Excellence is staffed with experienced Scrum and Kanban experts to mentor and coach the teams, seek Management support to align the teams with the vision and mission of the implementation, secure Executive sponsorship for organizational commitment in terms of funds and resources and engage the programmer community to internalize the model and make it part of the way of life.

Four forces for successful Pilot & Rollout

These four forces contribute to successful Scrumban implementation across the organization. However it is important to achieve positive outcomes from the pilot to encourage other teams to adapt Scrumban. The following figure outlines the phases between Pre-Pilot to Rollout, and their activities.

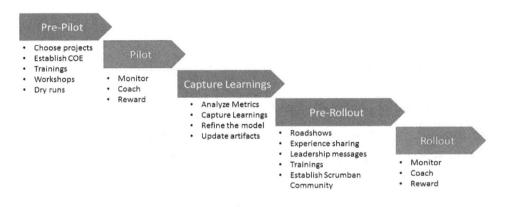

Pilot and Rollout phases

To make Pilot and Rollout smoother, there should be Pre-Pilot, Capture Learnings, and Pre-Rollout which prepares the ground and enables learning from the experience.

Pre-Pilot phase

Choosing the right pilot project or projects would help in foreseeing the rollout challenges ahead of time, so it is advised neither to choose easy projects nor tough projects. In parallel, the objectives of the Scrumban rollout must be defined in terms of outcomes.

Pre-Pilot

* Choose projects
* Establish COE
* Trainings
* Workshops
* Dry runs

The identified pilot team must undergo Scrumban training, participate in workshops to customize the processes and practices, and conduct dry runs to get familiarized with the model before they plunge in to the pilot.

Choose the right project for pilot

Choosing the right project for pilot is a crucial step to ensure a successful Scrumban rollout. It is easy to choose a project that is not very complex, but that would make the pilot successful without any learning needed to fine-tune the model. Choose a project that has good amount of complexity, but not something that would totally derail the confidence to go further. Here are some guidelines to help you choose the right one.

Right size: Choose a project that is small but not too small. It should have minimum of 10 and maximum of 20 team members. It is recommended not to choose large projects with more than 20 team members, these come with additional challenges which can be dealt later in the implementation journey.

Right scope: Make sure the types of work requests that are delivered by the project are mostly Software Maintenance work requests. Do not choose any mission critical software maintenance to be part of the pilot project. Choose a scope that allows the team to experiment and improvise. Some portion of the scope should be planned work and some part should be unplanned.

Right stakeholders: Make sure the product owner and project manager are willing to experiment. Adopting Scrumban requires changes on the business side of the stakeholders, not just the maintenance team. Someone on the business side who would want to experiment for the betterment of the delivery to be made as the key stakeholder.

Right team: Choose a project that has team with high appetite for innovative practices and high energy individuals with good team dynamics. Do not choose a project where the work is dependent on too many third-parties, other teams, or experts from other teams. At the same time, choose a project where there is some dependency from the third-parties to test the model.

Establish Center of Excellence

Establishing Center of Excellence (COE) is the most critical part of Scrumban journey. The identified team of experts to be part of the COE should not only have good Agile and Lean credentials and experience, they should also believe in Scrumban model. Without these experts having a good alignment with Scrumban vision and mission the COE will not be able to meet its purpose.

Establish Scrumban COE with three main objectives:

- To define Scrumban model as described in this publication, establishing practices, metrics & charts, and customizing the mode for your organization

- To provide content, tools & templates
- To coach and Mentor the teams

The four major responsibilities of Scrumban COE are:

1. Governance: COE should own the vision and mission of Scrumban set out for the organization and it should form the governance structure and underlying committees to ensure the strategic direction and mission is achieved. COE should be accountable for Scrumban OCM, but this function can be delegated to a specialized group to plan and execute the events, roadshows and workshops, with the subject matter expertise from COE.

2. Support: Scrumban COE should support all the projects implementing Scrumban. The support includes setting up of the model and customizing practices to suit the project requirements. COE should also provide coaching, mentoring, or subject matter experts to support the teams.

3. Knowledge Management: Scrumban COE should maintain the standards, methodologies, processes, practices, templates, and knowledge repositories.

4. Capability Building: COE should define the metrics to measure Scrumban performance, and support the teams to meet the performance goals set for all the metrics. COE should be conducting or coordinating the training and certifications, conducting skill assessments as part of the enablement cycle, and conducting any shared learning activities. COE should also play an

active role in forming the Scrumban community, and running it with active participation from all the stakeholders.

The COE plays a pivotal role in Scrumban implementation. It should be adequately staffed in order to execute the above functions. Some of the roles that must be in place as a beginning are below. Refine the staffing model as you go along. A well-established Scrumban COE is built from full and part-time resources:

1. Scrumban Masters: Scrumban Masters should have deep understanding of Scrum and Kanban and have good experience in playing this role for years.

2. Coaches or Senior Scrumban Masters: This role requires excellent knowledge and extensive experience in Lean and Agile methodologies, especially experience in paying Scrum Master role in diverse scenarios. It demands experience in coaching the teams with performance issues and other predicaments.

3. Analysts: This role demands a good understanding of the Quality Assurance process, quantitative project management, and procedures around measurements and metrics. An understanding of Scrumban would be an added advantage, they can be trained on Scrumban when they come onboard. The Analysts support the projects in measuring and analyzing the metrics performance across teams. These inputs would be vital for the teams as well as organization in improving the performance.

4. Leadership: Supporting a Scrumban COE are visionaries moderated by an enterprise prioritization and resource allocation process. These visionaries focus on expanding use of the competencies and challenging others to improve existing and explore new opportunities and relationships to keep the business relevant for an ever changing world.

Trainings

The pilot teams should go through the enablement cycle described above in this chapter. The team should go through the assessment, and based on the assessment their training needs should be identified. Training should be conducted according to the plan and should be followed by certification to complete the enablement cycle.

Workshops and Dry runs

After choosing the right project, the teams have to be trained on Agile and Lean methodologies, and the Scrumban model. It is very useful to have workshops where the pilot team(s), along with an expert moderator, would plan the transition from current practices to Scrumban practices. The entire transition should be visualized by the team and only moderated by the Scrumban master. This is a team activity to map their activities with Scrumban practices to create their version of Scrumban.

Pilot phase

It is mandatory to do pilot implementation of any model before implementing across the organization, unless it is only one or two projects being implemented.

```
                    ▶ Pilot
```

- Monitor
- Coach
- Reward

Pilot implementation involves experimenting with, learning, and refining the model to suit to your organization-specific scenario. This would lower the risk of failure, increase opportunities for feedback, confirm intended results, tailor needs specific to your scenario, increase buy-in from stakeholders, and validate the measurement and metrics.

Monitor from close quarters

Pilot implementation needs close monitoring from the leadership and management to provide all the organizational support in making it successful. Monitoring should increase motivation and enthusiasm, not scrutinize. There must be formal and informal channels to extract the feedback from the pilot team members and stakeholders to refine the proceedings and keep the pilot on track.

Coach from the sidelines

There are various types of coaching that should take place during the pilot implementation. The most important aspect of coaching is to develop skills and abilities to boot performance. Coaching is not to dictate the practices, or correct the mistakes, but to guide the teams to identify their own version of the model that meets Scrumban objectives. Coach from the sidelines.

Reward success never penalize

Pilot is not about successfully implementing Scrumban, it is to identify all the predicaments teams would face in implementing Scrumban, and to fine tune the model to suit organizational specific scenarios. In a way the goal is to fail early, and fail more, so that learning can be applied to improve the model. Success during pilot is not successful implementation, but failing and learning. Reward the pilot team, never penalize.

Stand by the team through thick and thin

The leadership need to stand by the pilot team through thick and thin. It is essential to pump enthusiasm and energy into the team from start to the end. A sense of pride and excitement should fuel the team through the pilot.

Capture Learnings Phase

This phase is mostly anchored by Center of Excellence, with activities such as gathering the pilot metrics and learning practices and procedures.

> Capture Learnings

- Analyze Metrics
- Capture Learnings
- Refine the model
- Update artifacts

Once data is collated from the pilot team, the analysis and refinement of the model should be conducted by a specialist or group of specialists who understand the model and the core structure of Scrumban. The guiding principle for the refinement is to keep the core purpose of implementing Scrumban intact while customizing Scrumban elements to suit your organization-specific scenarios.

Pre-Rollout phase

The Pre-Rollout phase is where most Organization Change Management activities happen. It should be planned and managed with a specialized OCM group within your organization, with support from the Center of Excellence.

Pre-Rollout

- Roadshows
- Experience sharing
- Leadership messages
- Trainings
- Establish Scrumban Community

Depending on the size and location of the developer community, roadshows should be conducted specific locations to ensure good coverage. Roadshows are designed to spread awareness on the Scrumban model and its benefits. It should illustrate the experience of pilot projects with videos and testimonies of the pilot team members. It would be even better to have at least one pilot team member interact with developer communities and share about the experience. Sharing the challenges in tandem with benefits would increase the credibility of the roadshows and allow the developer communities to embrace Scrumban model wholeheartedly.

Depending on the scale of the roll out, various events can be planned, such as quizzes, meet the expert, and seminars. It is also important to broadcast messages, preferably videos, to the community from your organization's senior leadership. This should create a encourage adoption of Scrumban. Similarly, training should be conducted in all locations with flexible dates and timings. The Scrumban community should be designed as one-stop shop for knowledge sharing, experience sharing, best practice sharing, expert support, discussion threads, and many other benefits of developer community.

Establish Scrumban Community

"When you're surrounded by people who share a passionate commitment around a common purpose anything is possible" quote by Howard Schultz summarizes the need for a Scrumban community. There is a need to have a place where individuals and teams who are passionate about continuously improving the model by learning from each other's experiences.

Like any other movement, sustenance is a big challenge if you don't know who your consumers are, and if you don't know who your members are then you can't sustain a developer community. Organization, leadership, and COE must communicate with the community or even bother to get to know them through the community.

Instead, the community is relegated to collaborating around a portal with discussion threads, it should be a central place where developers, managers, experts, and coaches come to share and learn about Scrumban. These communities also help the experts understand about the challenges on the ground, and help leadership gain a sense of their vision versus reality. Some of the aspects to be considered while forming a Scrumban community are given below. Refer to your organizational templates for such developer communities and design accordingly.

One-stop shop

Create a single platform, an extranet/intranet portal, if possible with a mobile interface. Unify the incoming and outgoing conversations, make it a one-stop shop experience for the community. Drive the Scrumban model deep in to the organization. Registrations and email subscriptions are the first obvious step in enabling community members to identify each other.

Thought leadership

One of the reasons for anyone to subscribe to the communities is to learn from the thought leaders in this field. Identify a thought leader either external or internal to your organization, get a commitment on a certain bandwidth from them to write blogs, answer queries, participate in discussion threads and other activities within the community.

Training needs

The community should enable the teams to meet their training needs, through providing information of trainings, links for registrations, access to training material, and also provide support to the team members to get certified.

Dedicated bandwidth from coaches and experts

Community should provide access to the coaches and experts who could answer queries, help teams with Scrumban related challenges, and bandwidth to review projects and suggest improvements.

Share Artifacts

All the Scrumban documentation on processes, practices, and metrics should be easily available on the community pages.

Showcase corner

It is essential to have a showcase of the successful implementations, or zero defect deliveries, successful Go-Live events to spread the positive messages to the community. These messages would reinforce the confidence levels of Scrumban teams.

Feedback

The feedback from your Scrumban community is just as important as feedback from your customers. Any feedback helps in making community services faster and more efficient. Issue tracking, feature requests, and queries with a good response framework are important to respond to all of the above in a reasonable timeframe.

Online portal with mobile interface

The community should be on an intranet site for everyone to access easily. The name of the community should be the shortcut to access the web portal. It has become mandatory to have a mobile interface for the portal so that it can be accessed anytime, anywhere on mobile devices, for greater engagement.

Rewards & Recognitions

Rewards and recognitions are one of the major factors that motivate team members to work harder and smarter. These could be tangible or intangible, within the team or across teams, but they must be timely in order to enthuse the team members. Applauding team members and teams for their achievements in front of their peers and others creates positive competition and helps the communities to be successful.

1. Institute prestigious awards at an organizational level to recognize the individuals and teams who delivered excellence through Scrumban. These should be handed in a large ceremony by someone senior in the organization.

2. Create a model for teams to recognize the expected behaviors and measure performances, to reward them with creative gifts or perks. These could be gift certificates or dinner coupons, anything that is tangible and motivates the team members to go the extra mile.

The objective is to recognize behaviors as well as outcomes, and reward team achievements over individual performance to foster team spirit.

Rollout phase

Whether it is a Big Bang rollout or Phased roll out across all the units or departments of your organization, fire up all the engines. The engines that need to be fired up are Center of Excellence, developer community, roadshows events, knowledge and enablement, and rewards and recognitions.

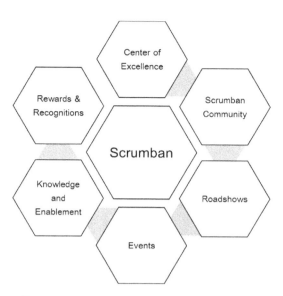

Engines to propel Scrumban movement

The teams should pull the Scrumban model to be their execution model than organization or COE pushing it to them. More than an organization wanting to implement Scrumban, teams should be wanting to adapt to improve Cycle Time and flow efficiency.

Institutionalization

The institutionalization of any process or practice should follow the quality triangle –Define, Measure, and Improve. The Quality Department of your organization will have a standard framework to institutionalize processes, practices, measurements, and metrics, which need to be communicated to the project teams. Metrics should be measured and baselined to compare with the standards.

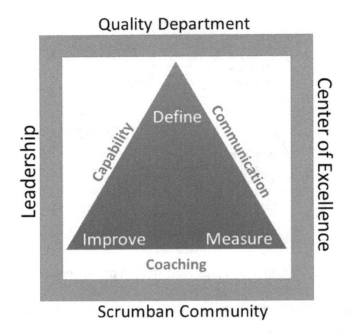

Institutionalization framework

The goals set for each of these metrics need to be achieved by the projects that implement Scrumban. These teams require coaching to improve their metrics performance. Based on the inputs from coaching, the team enabling programs need to be revised to improve the capabilities.

The quality triangle should be adequately supported by four organization functions. The first group is the Quality Department, defining, measuring, and improving the metrics. The second group is the Scrumban Center of Excellence, defining the practices and metrics, maintaining the communication with communities, and coaching the teams and building capabilities throughout the enablement cycle. The third group is the Scrumban community, engaging all stakeholders in the most efficient manner. The fourth group is the Leadership of the organization, sponsoring and directing to ensure institutionalization of Scrumban.

These are some of the additional steps needed to set sail on your Scrumban journey. Each of the topics are vast and need good amount of planning. This chapter only serves as a guideline to adopt to your organization-specific frameworks and practices.

***

Chapter 14

Final Words

"Somewhere, something incredible is waiting to be known." – Carl Sagan

Those were the five steps to implementing Scrumban in your project or organization. Scrumban is not just a model, it is a change of beliefs, a change in basic principles, and a change in fundamental practices. It is a paradigm shift and it is a cultural change. It may be a major shift in how your organization or your team operates, and could demand a significant amount of unlearning old and learning anew. It cannot be forced on teams. Organizations must understand the need to enable teams to unlearn, learn, and delve into this new cultural change, and must provide them with the necessary tools and systems. It must also support them with training and workshops to develop the skills.

Faux Scrumban

It is a very common trap, one that most organizations fall into, to have no alignment between leadership and team in the implementation of Scrumban. The team should believe in the principles and benefits from the start. Everyone in the team should be trained to understand the challenges of software maintenance work, and how Scrumban can help them focus more on work and improve their efficiency as individuals and as a team.

Certain important aspects of Scrumban are pivotal to achieve the real benefits of the model. For example, if the WIP limit is not enforced, the pull effect cannot be created, which results in each team member working on multiple requests or tasks. This results in stoppage of the work in hand and starting new work. Whenever there are multiple work requests and tasks on hand, switching contexts makes the team member inefficient. This in turn leads to higher Lead Times.

It is essential for any organization to align all the different layers of the organization structure and to understand and appreciate the principles and practices of Scrumban. These must be adhered to in order to gain the intended benefits.

Positive Thinking

Thinking positive might sound cliché in this day and age, and out of place in this publication for sure, but wouldn't to someone who is setting out on a new journey. When you are on a new path there are always challenges. Every step of the way raises questions about the new path you have taken. Whether it is the right model or not, whether the project is on the right track or not, whether something else is better than this model or not.

Every new journey poses challenges at every stage. As challenges arise, they need to be dealt in a timely manner and with a positive attitude. In most cases, something that may look negative can be turned into an opportunity for improvement. Never let any challenge bring you or the team down. Encourage the team to recognize a challenge and come up with improvements to make the model work for you.

For someone new to Scrum or Kanban models, self-management is often the most difficult part. This is where keeping a positive attitude is so important. Some of the things you try may not always work, but do not give up. It is easy to become downhearted. Team members should keep in mind that every bit of learning is important and that they are creating something that will enhance their efficiency as individuals and as a team.

Be respectful, but…

Although Scrumban principles recommend respecting the current processes, practices, and roles, there are certain new processes, practices, and roles that must be implemented to get the intended benefits. Respect the current processes, but make sure you tread on the path of change. Be merciless in stopping what is not needed and starting what is needed.

Find your own variation of Scrumban, and remember that the goal is to **stop starting and start finishing**.

***

www.ingramcontent.com/pod-product-compliance
Lightning Source LLC
Chambersburg PA
CBHW060551060326
40690CB00017B/3670